MA(

SUMERIAN SORCERY & THE DARK ARTS OF BABYLON

Edited & Introduced by Joshua Free
With Translation Assistance from Khem Juergen

The unpublished conclusion to the Tablet-M Series of the Necronomicon Anunnaki Bible. Released by the Mardukite Truth Seeker Press in 2011 as Liber-M – The NEW Maqlu Translation.

MAQLU MAGIC

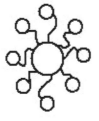

By Permission
of the Highest

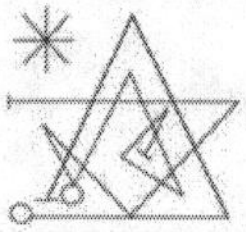

TABLE OF CONTENTS

MARDUKITE

MAQLU MAGIC

– Editor's Preface –

The MAQLU is perhaps one of the most interesting and profound aspects of – what some might consider '*Mesopotamian Magick*' or '*Babylonian Mysticism*'. It composes only one 'cycle' of a much 'Greater' *Mystery Tradition* and yet it has always been of considerable 'esoteric occult' and 'academic' value by itself – though it has gone wholly unrecognized as such. Some of this is of the fault of the current editor in past endeavors as well – and by saying this, an explanation is due.

As a 'translated' cycle of materials for inclusion in the work conducted by the early members of the *Mardukite Chamberlains Research Organization* in 2008 and 2009, the actually MAQLU (M-Series) of tablets were left unfinished – left in their *Babylo-Akkadian* transliteration for *eventual* translation. This period of time during the evolution of the 'reconstruction' of the complete 'Mardukite' legacy had been most heavily emphasized on the inner infrastructure of the civilization and the literature, often leaving the more 'practical' applications open for interpretation – regardless of how they were *actually* being conducted and executed within the chambers of the *Mardukite Home Office*. Such was left for 'later' or *eventual* interpretation by those who began to gain access publicly to what was at first only available to 'internal' members of the organization.

The M-Series is the only tablet cycle in the (eventually titled) *Necronomicon Anunnaki Bible* that is not in English. It had intended on being so for the 'original' Mardukite presentation of the *Liber N* (*Necronomicon*) – the first of many *libros* in the 'legacy', but debuting with a 'selection' of works from our 'Greater' *corpus* of materials that appeared to form a base for what many (*millions* in fact) had already come to know as the “Simon” *Necronomicon*. We were not 'reconstructing' the prior work, but instead reverse engineering from the 'source' the elements that the greater population would recognize. The *Liber N+L+G+9* anthology – now known the *Necronomicon Anunnaki Bible* – in its entirety, actually far surpasses anything that might have been gleaned from hermetic operation of the *Simonian* work prior – to even the most adept of your worldly *magicians and wizards*.

The original intention of our group back in the Spring of 2009 was to have the MAQLU translated and ready for what became one of our most momentous occasions in the history of the modern movement – the *Beltane 2009 StarGate Ceremony* – an event that resulted in our 'guidance' toward re-establishing the *Mardukite Chamberlains* movement publicly and under the guise of the "*Necronomicon.*" Prior to this 'event', such had never been considered fully.

What originally began as a mostly 'academic' or 'quasi-scientific' venture into *Anunnaki* and *Sumerian* topics had turned – what's more; the resources and 'museum-type' volunteers were increasingly disappearing from our fray as the mention of the word *Necronomicon* cropped up more and more. By late 2009 (correlating with the release of *Liber 9*) ALL extended relationships with 'academicians' had dissolved. It seemed that people were more than willing, even if only *anonymously*, to contribute assistance to a more rigorous 'Sitchinesque' or Daniken 'Ancient Alien' investigation than have anything to do with something connected to the *Necronomicon*...

What might have first appeared as the end of the world for our movement – leaving it just short of a two year run – turned into a moment for the internal staff (known as the *Council of Nabu-Tutu*) to look 'inward' and become more reflective. The acquisition of further 'source-materials' and 'translation' assistance would be difficult – if possible at all – forcing the 'Research & Development" efforts concentated more on interpretation and 'experimentation', leading to *Liber 50* (first released as *Gates of the Necronomicon* by Joshua Free and later to the public as *Sumerian Religion: Secrets of the Anunnaki*) as well as our own 'personal' contribution to the unique revival – *The Book of Marduk by Nabu*. In the midst of all this, the MAQLU was left behind, untranslated and unincorporated into the 'legacy' proper.

It was not out of neglect or oversight – it was simply unavailable...

We had begun to 'oversee' more of the work in mid-to-late 2009 at the *Home Office* directly, but it was not time enough for us to compile a 'Mardukite-approved' *Lexicon* of the language we were dealing with (a sampling of which can be found in the *Necronomicon Anunnaki Bible* as the Tablet-I Series). This meant that we were left mainly to ourselves if we wanted to see anything more done (beyond my own efforts on the *Book of Marduk by Nabu – Tablet W-Series* that was used privately by the inner order of the Chamberlains until its public release for Spring-Summer 2010 – correlating with the release of *Liber 50*).

Although further information and supplemental knowledge could be gathered on the MAQLU cycle – as was relayed in *Liber 9* and *Liber R* (also known as *Necronomicon Revelations*), the true incorporation of the MAQLU into the modern 'Mardukite' tradition could not be fully realized as we had originally hoped for...

...until NOW!

Dusting the tablets – and our own eyes – from a long-standing relationship with the desert sands, I am pleased to give the 'Mardukite' stamp of approval to what I hope will prove to be as incredible of an addition to your own treasure-trove of *Mesopotamian Mysteries* as it has been for me – an effort *many years* overdue.

~ NABU, JOSHUA FREE
Samhain – October 31, 2011
Mardukite Home Offices

MAQLU MAGIC

SUMERIAN SORCERY &
THE DARK ARTS OF BABYLON

The Dark Arts of Babylon

– An Introduction –

"Climb the ladder of lights
and appeal to the gods for their protection
and for the destruction of the enemy
and all evil-doers,
wicked witches and warlocks
of the world..."

– from the Tablet-M Series Preface
Necronomicon Anunnaki Bible

How often we have heard of the "Dark Arts" born of a 'polarized' and often 'dualistic' view of the universe – and the forces that occupy it. For every 'white witch' there is a 'black spell' and to every system of *Order*, there is a *Chaos* factor; for no fragmented experience of reality can ever actually find "balance", but the pendulum swing – the tidal ebb and flow of universal currents will always seek it. So, too is movement possible in the physical world – or at least one's perception of the '3-D' reality experienced. As such, with the once united 'crystal' being cracked into the varied refractions of human experience, language and culture, a 'dualistic' world emerged in consciousness; right before the very eyes of ancient *Mesopotamians* – at the heart and cradle of human civilization.

It is not the purpose of the current work to put forth the entire basis for the *Anunnaki* tradition among the ancients, or catalogue all of the historic *firsts* that arose in *Sumerian* culture 'as if from nowhere' or the legacy of the post-Sumerian *Babylonians* in the evolution of human civilization, societal order and 'belief systems' and their long-standing and far-sweeping affect on the planet and its populations – all of this has already been so concisely organized and offered in previous materials form the 'Mardukites'. For our present purpose we must fix our sights on a singular element of all of this – such as it applies to the MAQLU and the “Dark Arts” encountered in the ancient *Mardukite* system observed in *Babylon*.

This text can be understood well-enough as it stands and as it is being introduced, though it is suggested by the editor that reader-seeker who hopes to actually *implement* this operation into a reconstructive practice will benefit strongly from other works extended in the *Mardukite* legacy, including, but not limited to, *Necronomicon Anunnaki Bible* and the volumes that compose the *Gates of the Necronomicon* anthology: *Sumerian Religion*, *Babylonian Myth & Magic* and *Necronomicon Revelations*. For our present purposes, however, there will be sufficient background provided to grasp what purpose the MAQLU has – though within a much 'larger' or 'wide-angle' worldview, that is the "Anunnaki" perspective offered to us by the Sumerians and Babylonians coupled with the *oldest* writings on the planet in addition to the *oldest* source tradition that allowed the many other branches of the 'religio-spiritual' tree the spring up across space and time.

Firstly, the obvious question before the current editor is: *what is the MAQLU?* Before we can bring a reader's attention to the text itself, it seems appropriate that it should be introduced in such a way as can be appreciated by both the 'Mardukite Adept' and newcomer to the Mesopotamian Mysteries alike.

Before approaching the more 'colorful' elements of the tradition – those that could most appropriately be given classifications as 'Dark Arts', 'Sumerian Sorcery', 'Babylonian Witchcraft', 'magickal warfare' or 'wizards duels' – it is important that the *context* for which such exists, a background screen onto which to express the story of the MAQLU in its projected spectrum of rainbow lights and kaleidoscope glory.

The name MAQLU can be interpreted differently as with most things – such variegated perceptions are not even restricted to foreign languages for even a shared one is not free of *semantic issues* in its own vocabulary. Most typically, MAQLU is translated to mean "*the Burnings*" by '*Sumeriologists*' and such. This is a good 'base' for our context, as we do indeed find the origins of a community bonded for 'burning evil in effigy'. The *Simonian* work, in regards to a *Babylonian Necronomicon* practice, interprets the tablets as '*Rites of Burnt Offering*' or else a '*Book of Burnings*' for literary purposes. As with most of the work 'restored' by the *Mardukite Chamberlains*, a surface interpretation is never accepted and a 'deeper mystery' can often be uncovered in the very 'literal' meanings behind these very old words that do not appear to have had the same 'metaphorical' meaning that modern language users often take for granted – for the Mardukites have interpreted the MAQLU more appropriately – and not without its other diverse cultural parallels – as *Burning Man* [*maq-lu*].

Though it seems that the MAQLU operation was once a much more simple, internalized, meditative and solitary application used by early priests and magicians in *Mesopotamia*, it later developed more dramatically as a public *Fire Festival* in Sumer and Babylonia, involving the entire population of the community who gathered together in a 'combined' and 'harmonic' effort of intention to 'drive out' or 'dispel' the "evil" and "evil-doers" of the land. As "ridiculous" as this might sound to the naïve skeptic or right-wing fundamentalist, it can and should be noted that more recent public scientific studies all over the globe have now shown the effective abilities of consciousness moving energies when large groups, or better, the majority of the population has been focused on a specific 'emotional' event. These types of 'quantum' effects appear to have very real ramifications for the population of the planet and the greater cosmos as a whole in this entangled universe whether or not people are even aware of this phenomenon taking place in their environment and even internal 'spirito-mental' being (which are *self-honestly* all-as-One).

In the instance of the MAQLU, the *Burning Man* is the representation of the 'evil-doers' of the world – those who 'plagued' humanity with their wickedness and thereby upsetting the 'world order' of the *gods*, in addition to the *gods* themselves. Upsetting such a balance was usually felt in the community as 'illness' and 'pestilence', 'disease' and 'famine'. Such could prove devastating to still developing human civilizations, and as such they were considered 'evil', the most wicked of 'demons' and anything that might lead to them – mostly uncleanliness and misappropriated living – were considered taboo (the original non-moral tribal sins) and for good reason. For example, eating from an unclean plate was taboo (a sin) because it could lead to the spread of disease. Ancient humans were far from *primitive* in their understanding of the natural world and their relationship with it. Before the wrongful use of authority in classical times, the taboos and sins were not given from dogma, but from medicinal necessity.

Representative images are often used in 'idol magic' or 'sympathetic magic', but not as a result of worship – as some mythographers have repeatedly put forth – but to actually embody the 'energetic current' that is universally entangled to 'focal object' and its form. For example, the representation of a 'demon', e.g. the 'plague-god' *Namtaru*, was not to worship the deity with homage or to glorify the 'daemonology' of the Babylonian priests. Such statuary was typically constructed only to be 'ceremonially' annihilated or buried as a 'ward' against what the statue (deity) was representative of. In making such an object, the magicians show their understanding of the 'entanglement' of the universe in its mystical oneness and the interconnection of all things. Certainly not *primitive.*

It is almost impossible to bring up the topic of the *Burning Man* without conjuring to mind a much more geographical and time-recent example made popular in the images of motion pictures and familiar Roman-inspired writings of the *Celtic Druids* – and that is the *Wicker Man*, also called '*Burning Man*' by some neopagans. Far removed in time and space we see evidence for the same rite being conducted and for similar reasons – the preservation of the early agricultural civilizations that were 'guided' by *Sky God* traditions – called the *Anunnaki* on *Mesopotamian tablets* or the Tuatha de Dannan (*Tuatha d'Anu*) in *European* sources.

"Fire" is a very common element to the early 'magical' and 'shamanic' systems, and its mastery in correlation to the development of modern humans is certainly *undisputable.* Any connection to the *Fire Festivals* of Europe is going to be difficult for one to understand without having been familiarized to the rigorous research found in other *Mardukite* materials that gives *Mesopotamia* as the birthplace of the *Druidic Tradition* (see also *Liber D*, found in *Druids of the Deep* and *Book of Elven-Faerie* as well as *Draconomicon*). But it is a worthwhile pursuit for those interested in such a connection. Sir Francis Frazer (*Golden Bough*) mentions both a 'solar' alignment and 'purification' style to these types of operations. The later *European Wicker Giants* appear to be more 'agricultural' in nature then the MAQLU version that targets actual 'practitioners' of the 'Dark Arts' that negatively affect the well-being of the greater population, the community at large and by extension the "moral balance" perceived of 'universal forces'.

The ancient *Sumerians* and *Babylonians* were no less dependent on the 'agricultural' fertility then the *Celts* – far from it. Thriving of a human numbers in the lands of *Mesopotamia* were so heavily dependent on the skilled use of arid land and the redirection of water from the *Tigris* and *Euphrates* rivers in a skillful way since lost to the Arabs and other occupiers of the land since. In *Europe*, we find the appearance of the *Burning Man* during the fertile and seed-sowing and nurturing 'spring' seasons, particularly the Equinox (Easter) observation, *Beltane* (a notorious '*Fire Festival*') and finally *Midsummer*. The annual survival of the agricultural *Celts* was wholly dependent on the success of this season above all others.

Life in *Mesopotamia* and its seasons were somewhat different – but they best correlate to two times that the MAQLU and other large public festival appearances seem to occur. One of which *does* correlate with *Europe* is an esoteric observation of *Beltane* – opposite it, *Samhain* (modern-day *Halloween*) is also significant. The *Sumerio-Babylonian* AKITU festival is concurrent with the Spring Equinox. So, regardless of where we turn, there is a unifying (universal) picture forming to define the ceremonial observation of the *Burnings*.

A "True" Necronomicon Spellbook

– The Magick of the Maqlu –

"More than simply the exorcism of evil spirits,
or a manual to anti-demon healing rites –
the MAQLU is meant to target those
who feed "evil" its existence:
the wicked witch and evil sorcerer."

– from Liber-R (Joshua Free)
Necronomicon Revelations

The noted appearance of the MAQLU extracts for the "Simon" *Necronomicon* left many in wonder (or not) as to what *more* might appear behind the curtains of Babylonian mysticism. Although the origins of this method may have indeed been found among the *Sumerians*, the operation as it appears here (and from what most other common depictions are derived from) is wholly a Babylonian recension – a *Mardukite* masterpiece of ceremonial ritualism. Naturally – the *Necronomicon* offered only a 'part' of a greater literary cycle, just as was seen with the *Simonian* renderings of the *Enuma Elis* and *Descent of Ishtar* among others.

The 'initiatory' focus of the *Simon* work caused many to overlook what the MAQLU really was. In spite of the 100 incantations it later developed to be, only a dozen appear in the popular edition; their pretense being a sort of 'protective' "counter-magic" to battle those who, in the dualistic perspective, are in alignment (or worship) "Ancient Ones" who are perceived to be evil – and the source of the evil-doers power.

It is possible that the selections found in the *Simonian* work are simply reflections of an older and simpler version of the same rite; one which was originally performed on a more 'astral' level of consciousness – though with the same 'effect' and 'purpose'. Later, the MAQLU became a lengthier, more complex and public affair, meant to soothe the 'group mind' or 'consciousness' of the people and their own 'astral' or 'auric' defenses against the 'Dark Arts'.

In addition to the popular *Necronomicon*, there are common elements of the incantations that many occultists and esoteric magicians will find reminiscent to other *Arabic*, *Semitic*, *Assyrian*, *Hebrew* and related systems. In every instance, the incantations are used for 'healing' magic or to drive away 'evil spirits'. But more than simply combating the entities and energies directly, the MAQLU focuses on the practitioners who feed these currents of power their existence (via participation and belief) while at the same time feeding off of or deriving energy channeled from these currents that appear to be 'negative' in polarity when clashed against the 'reality' of the 'Realm'.

Without duplicating the numerous volumes of preparatory 'Mardukite' materials available to a *seeker* who desires to implement the MAQLU methodology in their own practices – concerning the preparation of the practitioner (internal set) and the environment (external setting), there are a few facets specifically appearing in reenactments of the MAQLU in modern times that can be included here in repose.

The mystical 'correspondence' related to the operation of the MAQLU is indeed what some would call the "Dark Arts", but it is forgiving in that the purpose of its 'study' and 'use' in this respect is to 'battle' such practices that are destructive or chaotic to the community.

Where most traditions connected to these types of practices – at least as they are observed today – are in fact mainly 'passive' and wholly 'of the shield', the MAQLU provides the stoic and dedicated priest-magicians of the *state* a 'power of the sword'. The MAQLU represents the archetypal epitome of 'fighting *fire with fire*' such as is actually quite unique in truly historical arcana. Perhaps the phrase has no greater esoteric application then to the MAQLU *Burnings*.

Given the orientation of the working, the traditional dressings (of the practitioners and the altar) are black. An 'element' of purple is also incorporated if the dedication of the rite is truly to MARDUK – for it is *his* color. The color black is significant to the 7th step or highest level of the 'fragmentation' or 'gates' of the material world, traditionally aligned to *Saturn* (and to NINURTA-NINIB). This current, coupled with the usurped-Jupiter power by

MARDUK for the "Younger Generation" of *Anunnaki*, is what enables the Babylonian (*Mardukite*) operator the ability to execute the MAQLU... "for the incantation is the incantation of MARDUK", meaning that the power to conduct the rituals of Babylon were a birthright given to the priestly and kingly lineages 'from the heavens' (*Anunnaki*) or in this case the 'blood of MARDUK' (which is to say the *Race of Marduk*) or 'dragonblood' that ran in the blood of magicians and rulers most purely during the antiquated development of human civilization. [See also *Liber D.*]

In the case of the MAQLU, it is said that it should be "performed by the pure offspring of the Deep", which is again a reference to the *Mardukites* proper. The "Deep" is a direct reference to the 'abode of ENKI' and the original birthplace of 'magick' on earth – by extension MARDUK becomes the first 'priest of Eridu' (the home-city of ENKI on earth) and the mysteries are eventually based down to the later Babylonian (Mardukite) priest-scribes by way of NABU (son of MARDUK).

Many of the applications call for the preparation of a 'portable temple' if such is not being performed *within* an actual temple. This is one of the original sources for the 'casting of a circle' that we see so common in the later 'stolen' fragmentations of the root tradition. At first, *all* "magic" was the possession of the priests who served the *gods* and it was not known among the people (or even witnessed) in any way. As a result it was easy to conceal all practices in the 'temples' or 'shrines' (very of *ziggurats* or *pyramids*), places which were already 'consecrated' (literally 'touched and changed') by the *gods* directly! This element of 'mobile magic' developed much later when it 'came down' to the people and their 'perceptive' interpretations of 'mysticism'.

Some of the most common and almost 'shamanic' styled methods of consecrating 'sacred space' for the MAQLU can be found among the descriptions of the *usurtu*, commonly translated to mean '*mandala*' or '*magic circle*'. The sprinkling of *lime* is mentioned frequently in many *Mesopotamian* texts and circles themselves (as well as any other 'glyphs' and 'symbols' incorporated) are typically marked on the ground with the 'Flour of Nisaba' (*Sumerian*) or 'Flour of Nabu' (*Babylo-Mardukite*).

May Marduk,
Eldest Son of Eridu
Sprinkle the afflcted nation
with pure water,
Clean water, Bright water,
With the water, twice seven times,
That we may be made pure and clean;
Let the evil Rabisu [daemons] go forth
and stand away from us!
May a kindly Sedu [spirit]
and a kindly Lamasu [guardian]
Come forth and be present among us!

Babylonian Witchcraft

– The Division of Power –

"Ceremonial burnings in metaphoric effigy are usually performed with waxen dolls 'made in the image of your enemy.' Elsewhere translations explain that 'a waxen doll may be cursed over a flame and then melted' into a cauldron."

– <u>Mardukite Wizards of the Wastelands</u>

The practice of magic, in and of itself, was not at all criminal in *Mesopotamia* – a cultural land that was not foreign to the ideas of the occult. Magic was, however, the function of the state, or that is to say the Realm; specifically the priests, kings and magicians of the Realm who were responsible enough and charged by 'Divine Right' to execute the 'magical arts'.

What is generally available to *seekers* now, after thousands of years of fragmentation, cultural separation, paradigm formations and other various *grimoires* – is but a *shadow* of the 'real magic' that was known to the ancients that worked side-by-side along with their own *Sky Gods*. And *such* was its originating purpose on the planet. It is the misinformed efforts of later humans that has, in essence, corrupted the 'sacred arts' of "magick". But it is not the placement of blame that we seek; it matters little *who* is at fault - only that the issue is rectified.

Priestly-magic was considered 'divine' or 'tr-anscendental', given to the *Races* as a birth-right; sacred and not to be taken for granted. The education and use of these arts were a closely guarded secret among the most anci-ent factions who were all connected to the 'Sky God' traditions. Included (and most anci-ent) among these was the Brotherhood of the Snake (or Serpent) [or *Ancient Ones*] that was later divided into polar-dualism on the plan-et and realized as Orders of the Dragon. While they remain unified in their origins, each of the various 'sects' was given only a limited understanding (perceptual experien-ce) of the All-as-One...

Doing so prevented the total 'universal control' of reality outside of unification (unity). But this did not guarantee a *perfect* system, for in its perfection there lies dormant always the *chaos* factor. And to this is answered the MAQLU – at least by *Mesopotamian* standards.

Given the language used to describe the evil-doers in the MAQLU, it seems that the *seeker* also uncovers the origins of the 'division of class magic' and the disapproving 'labels' given to the practitioners dedicated to the 'Dark Arts' for malignant purposes. Rather than put the self-honest priest-magician at risk of 'turning to the Dark Side', the MAQLU allows the *Mardukite* to petition the *Anunnaki* to execute such actions on their behalf. The nature of the work – though still considered 'Dark Arts' – is then transferred away from the operator (in terms of karmic or energetic repercussions) and taken up by the 'divine' intermediary'. By appealing to the 'Highest', the one who is in alignment (in this case it is assumed the self-honest priest) with *cosmic order* will prevail. So as not to be left defenseless against the malicious acts capable of evil-doers, the 'blessed' community is given the MAQLU and any effect is believed to be in 'self-defense' and by 'divine ordinance'.

The terms 'wicked witch' and 'evil sorcerer' appear frequently in the MAQLU to define the practitioners of the 'Dark Arts', evil-doers or 'Worshipers of the Ancient Ones' (depending on your preference). Though the polarity of power does not appear present in the original worldview (proto-Sumerian) and that which pertains to the *Supernal Trinity* (ANU, ENLIL and ENKI), by the time the MAQLU makes its presence in Babylon around 4,000 years ago, the division of power into 'polarity' and 'fragmentation' has already taken place in programmed human society. These terms are not meant to relay anything specifically derogatory by 'modern' *New Age* standards, but they do reflect what the ancient *Mesopotamian* attitude was in regards to the practice of magic. For our (simplified) purposes, the operation by priest-scribes and court-magicians of the Realm was acceptable – the 'borrowing' of practices by the commoners, peasant and folk-class, resigned members of the temple and others outside the Realm was considered 'wrong' for more purposes than can be fully clarified within the current text. For this work, it would suffice to say that the secrecy of the art was to prevent exactly what the MAQLU exists to overcome – the ill-use of magic by one's standing apart from 'society'.

Using the *Mardukite* standards of operation, the MAQLU is conducted by 'Divine Right' and via the 'incantation of MARDUK'. This means that all the 'fundamental' elements of a truly *Mardukite* ritual would apply. Among these is the acknowledgment of the 'usurped power' taken by MARDUK for Babylonians as described in the *Enuma Elis* – Creation cycle of tablets (found in the *Necronomicon Anunnaki Bible*). It was not uncommon for this 'myth' to be told during such festival ceremonies as a means of demonstrating the basis for the 'authority' and 'power' being executed in the rite. When the ritual was conducted in Erech and by the 'followers of Inanna-Ishtar', it was tradition to retell her 'underworld' cycle as a means of demonstrating her 'supreme' abilities. In such ways the 'hierarchical' methodologies of magick came to be born, best seen in their later evolutions in Greco-Egyptian Hermeticism.

The occult means by which the MAQLU primarily operates is known in anthropology as 'sympathetic magic' or 'transference'; in this case, the 'transference of evil'. Such practices are typical of indigenous and 'mystical' cultures around the globe, all containing aspects that can be traced back to the MAQLU and its alignment to the *Sky Gods* or *Anunnaki*.

In the original descriptions of the MAQLU, the *Mardukite* is shown the 'ladder of lights' on which they must 'ascend' in order to appeal to the *Anunnaki*, that they might offer their powers to the occasion – the *burning of evil*. This reference to an initiatory methodology of pathwork (sometimes referred to as *gate-walking*, *gatekeeping* or *starwalking*) is a part of the 'preparations' of the priest-magician, thought to have been 'worked through' long prior to the execution of the MAQLU; meaning the operator is expected to have already 'traversed' the *Gates* and developed a relationship with the *Anunnaki* (*Sky Gods*).

In addition to a *burnt offering* representative of the 'evil-doers', the ceremony also invites the appearance of 'seven idol' statues of the *Seven Anunnaki* found in the Babylonian (or Mardukite) paradigm; e.g. *the seven* deities that represent the *Gates* of *Babili*: Nanna-Sin, Nabu, Inanna-Ishtar, Shammash, Nergal, Marduk and Ninurta. The presence of *burasu* (juniper/cypress), *binu* (dragon's blood) and *mastakal* (semen) also appear to be mentioned in the guides for Babylonian ritual magic, however the practitioner might interpret these things today.

THE MAQLU

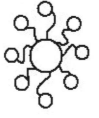

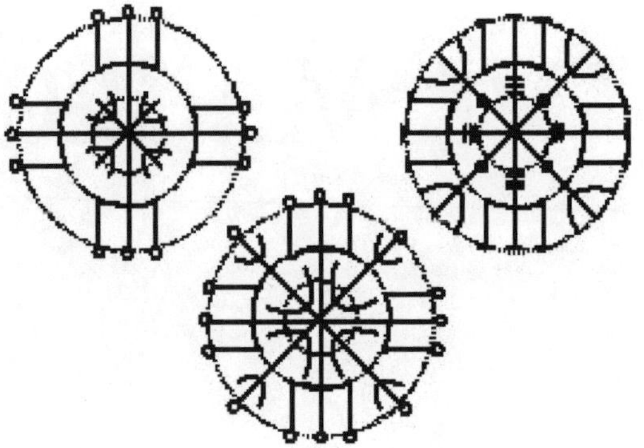

TABLET I

ÉN[*] *al-si-ku-nu-ši ilimeš mu-ši-ti*
I call upon you, Gods of Night
it-ti-ku-nu al-si mu-ši-tum kal-la-tum ku-túm-tum
With you, I call upon the Night, the Veiled Lady
al-si ba-ra-ri-tum qab-li-tum u na-ma-ri-tum
I call at twilight, midnight and dawn,
áš-šú kassaptuú-kaš-šip-an-ni
Because the sorcerer has enchanted me,

e-li-ni-tum ub-bi-ra-an-ni
A [sorceress] has spoken against me,
ili-ia ù distar-ia ú-šis-su-ú eli-ia
Causing my god and goddess to distance from me;
elî a-me-ri-ia am-ru-u a-na-ku
I am a pathetic sight to behold,
im-di-ku la a-la-lu mûša ù ur-ra
I am unable to rest day or night
qu-ú im-ta-na-al-lu-ú pî-ia
and a gag has filled my mouth

ú-pu-un-ti pi-ia ip-ru-su
food has been kept from my mouth
mêmeš maš-ti-ti-ia ú-ma-u-ú
the water ceases to enter my throat;

---

* General Key: "EN" is indicative of *incantation*. SU.EN or TU.EN generally translated as *incantation formula*. They mainly serve to divide the 'separate' incantations found within the greater text of the MAQLU. To avoid the unnecessary – the terms described will not be repeated throughout the body of the transliteration. ~ *trans.* K.J.

e-li-li nu-bu-ú hi-du-ti si-ip-di
my praise is lament, my rejoice is sorrow:
i-zi-za-nim-ma ilimeš rabutimeš ši-ma-a da-ba-bi
stand by my side, Great Gods, give me notice,
di-ni di-na a-lak-ti lim-da
be a judge in my case, grant me a decision.

e-pu-uš alam amelkaššapi-ia u kaššapti-ia
I formed an image of my sorcerer and sorceress,
šá e-piš-ia u muš-te-piš-ti-iar
of my enchanter and enchantress;
áš-kun ina šap-li-ku-nu-ma a-dib-bu-ub di-ni
I have laid them in fire and await your judgment;
áš-šú i-pu-šá lim-ni-e-ti iš-te-'-a la ba-na-a-ti
because [they] have conjured evil against me:
ši-i li-mut-ma a-na-ku lu-ub-lut
may [they] die, that I can live!

kiš-pu-šá ru-hu-šá ru-sú-u-šá lip-pa-áš-ru
The evil magick, the evil spell must be broken!
ibînu lil-lil-an-ni šá qim-ma-tú ša-ru-ú
The [*Tamarisk*] Crown of ANU purifies me!
igišimmaru lip-šur-an-ni ma-hi-rat ka-lu-ú šáru
The [datepalm] catching all the wind, frees me!
šam-maštakal li-bi-ban-ni šá iritimtim ma-la-a-ta
The [*maskatal*] shines through me, filling the earth.
terînatu lip-šur-an-ni šá še-am ma-la-a-ta
The [pinecone] full of seeds, frees me!

ina mah-ri-ku-nu e-te-lil ki-ma šamsassati
In front of you I have become light as grass;
e-te-bi-ib az-za-ku ki-ma la-ar-di
I am shinning and pure like grass.

tu-ú-šá šá kaššapti li-mut-te
The spell of the [sorceress] is baneful;
tu-ur-rat amât-sa ana pî-šá lišân-šá qa-a-rat
Let [her] words fall in her mouth, tongue-tied!
in elî kiš-pi-šá lim-ha-u-ši ilimeš mu-ši ti
Let the Gods of Night overcome [her] spell.

maarâtimeš šá mu-ši lip-šu-ru ru-hi-šá lim-nu-ti
Let the Three Watchers overcome the evil spell.
pú-šá lu-ú lipû lišân-šá lu-ú âbtu
Let [her] words be dust and tongue turned to salt,
šá iq-bu-ú amât limutimtim-ia ki-ma lipî lit-ta-tuk
which spoke the baneful formula, come to dust!
šá i-pu-šú kiš-pi ki-ma âbti liš-har-mi
The magick, let it dissolve like salt!
qi-is-ru-šá pu-u-u-ru ip-še-tu-šá hul-lu-qú
The knots are undone, [her] efforts are destroyed,

kal a-ma-tu-šá ma-la-a êra
All [her] words fill the void
ina qi-bit iq-bu-ú ilimeš mu-ši-tum SU.EN
by the covenant that the Gods of Night decreed!

ÉN irsitumtum irsitumtum irsitumtum-ma
Earth! Earth! Ye Spirit of the Earth
dgilgameš BEL ma-mi-ti-ku-nu
[Gilgamesh] is the lord of your course!
min-mu-ú at-tu-nu te-pu-šá ana-ku i-di
What has befallen you, I know:

[40] min-mu-ú ana-ku ip-pu-šu at-tu-nu ul ti-da-a
What has befallen me, you know not yet.
min-mu-ú kaššapatimeš-ia ip-pu-šá e-ga-a-pa-ti-ra pa-šir lâ irašši SU.EN
What the [sorceress] has let loose on me, no one can undo; it has no undoer!

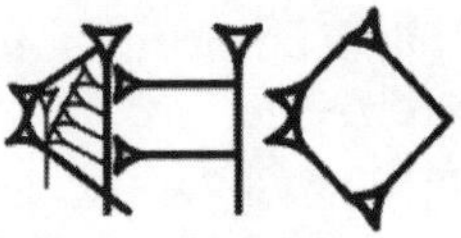

ÉN ali-ia zab-ban ali-ia zab-ban
My city is [Zabban]. My city is [Zabban].
šá ali-ia zab-ban-ta abullatimeš-šú-it
My city of [Zabban] has two Gates:
ana sit dšamši šá-ni-tu ana erib dšamši-it
The first is on the east, the second on the west.

[45] ana si-it dšamšiši šá-ni-tu ana e-rib dšamšiši
One is for the sunrise, one is for the sunset.
a-na-ku e-ra ha-as-ba šam-maštakal na-šá-ku
I am lifting to you my seed [*maskatal*].
a-na ilimeš šá šamêe mêmeš a-nam-din
To the Sky Gods I bring water.
kîma ana-ku ana ka-a-šú-nu ul-la-lu-ku-nu-ši
As do I come to purify you
at-tu-nu ia-a-ši ul-li-la-in-ni SU.EN
so come forth to purify me!

ÉN ak-la ni-bi-ru ak-ta-li ka-a-ru
I have barred-up the river-crossing and harbor,
ak-li ip-ši-ši-na šá ka-li-ši-na ma-ta-a-ti
I hold back the magick of all lands;
da-nim u an-tum iš-pu-ru-in-ni
ANU and ANTU have sent me here
man-nu lu-uš-pur a-na dbe-lit sêri
but whom should I send to BELIT-SERI?

ana pî lúkaššapi-ia u kaššapti-ia i-di-i hur-gul-li
In the mouth of the evil warlock and witch, gag!
i-di-i šipat-su šá apqal ilimeš MARDUK
By the incantation of the Magician God, MARDUK!
lil-sa-ki-ma la tap-pa-li-ši-na-a-ti
They will call upon you, but do not answer them;
liq-ba-nik-ki-ma la ta-šim-me-ši-na-a-ti
They will come before you, but do not listen to them.
lu-ul-si-ki-ma a-pu-ul-in-ni
Only should I call to you, should you answer me:
lu-qu-ba-ki-ma ši-min-ni ia-a-ti
Should I come before you, should you listen to me,

ina qí-bit iq-bu-u da-nim an-tum u dbe-lit sêri SU.EN
And to the covenant that ANU, ANTU and BELIT-SERI have issued!

ÉN šap-ra-ku al-lak '-ú-ra-ku a-dib-bu-ub
Where I am sent, I go. When ordered, I speak:
a-na li-it lúkaššapi-ia u kaššapti-ia dasar-lú-du-BEL a-ši-pu-ti iš-pur-an-ni
Against the evil sorcerer and sorceress *Asalluhi* [MARDUK], Lord of the Incantation, has sent me.
šá šamê qu-la šá irsitimtim ši-ma-a
Take note of what is in sky and on earth!
šá nâri qu-la-ni šá na-ba-li ši-ma-a amât-su
Take note of what is in the river and the word spoken on land!

[65] šaru na-zi-qu tur-ru-uk e tal-lik
Wind, carrier of lightning, strike it down!
šá gišhatti u gišmar-te-e tur-ru-uk e tal-lak
The stick [image] is now broken, break it!
li-iz-zi-iz har-ra-an mârat ilimeš ra-butimeš
Let them stand waiting at the Gateway to the Gods
a-di a-mat lúkaššapi-ia u kaššapti-ia a-qab-bu-ú
until I speak the Word to my evil sorcerer and wicked witch.
šu'u i-pa-áš-šar immeru i-pa-áš-šar
The lamb will be freed! The sheep will be freed!

[70] a-mat-su-nu lip-pa-šir-ma a-ma-ti la ip-pa-áš-šar
Their words may be loosened, but my Word will not be.
a-mat a-qab-bu-ú a-mat-su-nu ana pân amâti-ia lâ iparrik
The Word that I speak, their words cannot withstand it!
ina qi-bit dasari-lú-du BEL a-ši-pu-ti SU.EN
By the covenant of the Lord of the Incantations!

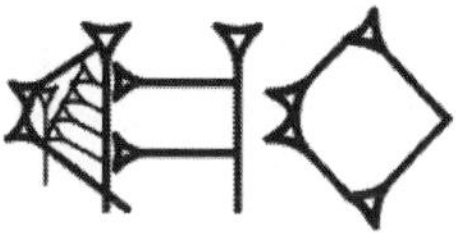

ÉN NUSKU an-nu-tum salmânimeš e-piš-ia
NUSKU, these [images] are of my evil sorcerer.
an-nu-ti salmânimeš e-piš-ti-ia
These [images] are of my wicked sorceress;

salmânimeš lúkaššapi-ia u kaššapti-ia
These [images] are of my warlock and witch,
salmânimeš e-piš-ia u muš-te-piš-ti-ia
These [images] are of my enchantress,
salmânimeš sa-hir-ia u sa-hir-ti-ia
These [images] are of my stuifier,
salmânimeš ra-hi-ia u ra-hi-ti-ia
These [images] are of my bewitchment,
salmânimeš BEL ik-ki-ia u BELIT ik-ki-ia
These [images] are of my lord and lady opponent,

salmânimeš BEL sir-ri-ia u BELIT sir-ri-ia
These [images] are of my lord and lady enemy.
salmânimeš BEL ri-di-ia u BELIT ri-di-ia
These [images] are of my lord and lady prosecutor.
salmânimeš BEL di-ni-ia u BELIT di-ni-ia
These [images] are of my lord and lady accuser.
salmânimeš BEL amâti-ia u BELIT amâti-ia
These [images] are of my lord and lady slanderer.
salmânimeš BEL daba-bi-ia u BELIT daba-bi-ia
These [images] are of my lord and lady defector.

salmânimeš BEL egirri-ia u BELIT egirri-ia
These [images] are of my lord and lady nemesis.

salmânimeš BEL limutti-ia u BELIT limut-ti-ia
These [images] are of my lord and lady evil-doer.
NUSKU da-a-a-nu tidu-šú-nu-ti-ma ana-ku la i-du-šú-nu-ti
NUSKU, only you know them. I do not know them,

šá kiš-pu ru-hu-u ru-su-u up-šá-še-e lim-nu-ti
their trick, their magick, their evil spells,
ip-šá bar-tum a-mat li-mut-ti râmu zêru
sorceries, manipulations, evil words, love, hate,

[90] dipalaa zitarrutâa kadibbidâa kúš-hunga
lying, murdering, confounding the truth of words,
šabalbalâa su-ud pa-ni ša-ni-e tè-mu
untrusting, quick to anger, lacking wisdom,
ma-la ibšu-u-ni is-hu-ru-ni u-šá-as-hi-ru-ni
everything that they have drawn to them,
an-nu-tum šú-nu an-nu-ti salmânimeš-šu-nu
these are those things; these are their [images],
kima šu-nu la iz-za-az-zu salmânimeš-šu-nu na-šá-ku
because the [images] cannot stand up, I lift them toward you,

[95] at-ta NUSKU u ANU ka-šid lim-nu u a-a-bi kušus-su-nu-ti-ma ana-ku la ah-hab-bil
NUSKU and ANU, you who captures enemies, catch mine before I am destroyed!
šá salmânimeš-ia ib-nu-u bu-un-na-an-ni-ia ú-maš-ši-lu
Those others that make my [images] and mimic my form,
pani-ia ú-sab-bi-tú kišâdi-ia ú-tar-ri-ru
they attack my face, they tie up my neck,
irti-ia id-i-bu esemti-ia ik-pu-pu
they hit my chest, they bend up my back.

a-hi-ia un-ni-šu ni-iš lib-bi-ia is-ba-tu
they make my arms weak and remove my strength,

lib-bi ilimeš itti-ia ú-za-an-nu-ú emûqi-ia un-ni-šu
they make the Spirit of the Lord angry with me and removed my strength,
li-it a-hi-ia iš-pu-ku bir-ki-ia ik-su-ú
they stripped the strength from my arms, and my knees are plagued with pain,
man-ga lu-'-tú ú-mal-lu-in-ni
they cause me to faint,
akâlemeš kaš-šá-pu-ti ú-šá-ki-lu-in-ni
they cause me to eat accursed food,
mêmeš kaš-šá-pu-ti iš-qu-in-ni
they cause me to drink foul water,

rim-ki lu-'-ti ú-ra-me-ku-in-ni
they have purified me with unclean water,
nap-šal-ti šam-me lim-nu-ti ip-šu-šu-in-ni
they have washed me in juice of unclean seeds,
ana lúmiti i-hi-ru-in-ni
they have mocked me as though I am dead,
mêmeš napištimtim-ia ina qab-rì uš-ni-lu
they have placed my spirit among the dead,
ilu šarru BELU u rubû it-ti-ia ú-za-an-nu-ú
they have made my god, king and master angry with me;

at-ta GIRRA qa-mu-ú lúkaššapu u kaššaptu
GIRRA [*Fires of God*] who burns the evil warlock and witch,
mu-hal-liq rag-gi zêr lúkaššapi u kaš-šapti
Who slays the evil offpsring of the warlock and witch,

mu-ab-bit lim-nu-ti at-ta-ma
Who slays the evil-doers? It is You!
ana-ku al-si-ka ki-ma SAMAS u ANU
I call upon you like SAMAS [*Shammash*] and ANU
di-i-ni di-ni purussâ-ai purusus
Make me right, be the judge of my decision!

qu-mu lúkaššapu u kaššaptu
Burn the evil sorcerer and sorceress!
a-kul ai-bi-ia a-ru-uh lim-nu-ti-ia
Be the eater of my enemies, consume all those who wish me evil!
ûm-ka iz-zu lik-šu-šu-nu-ti
May they catch your roaring flames!
ki-ma mêmeš nâdi ina ti-qi liq-tu-ú
May their lives end like sewage!
ki-ma ti-rik abnêmeš ubânâtimeš-šú-nu liq-ta-as-si-sú
May their fingers be wrecked like those of stone-masons, chewed off!

ina qi-bi-ti-ka sir-ti šá lâ innakaruru
By the name of the Glorious Command
ù an-ni-ka ki-nim šá lâ innennuú SU.EN
and your Everlasting Covenant!

ÉN NUSKU šur-bu-ú i-lit-ti da-nim
NUSKU, Mighty Offspring of ANU
tam-šil abi bu-kur den-lil
True [image] of your father, firstborn of ENLIL,

tar-bit apsî bi-nu-ut dBEL šamêe irsitim
Son of the Abyss, Son of the Lord of Heaven-Earth

[125] áš-ši tipâra ú-nam-mir-ka ka-a-šá
I lift the torch and illuminate you,
lúkaššapu ik-šip-an-ni kiš-pi ik-šip-an-ni ki-šip-šú
The wicked sorcerer who has cursed me, curse him with the spell [he] used on me!
kassaptutak-šip-an-ni kiš-pi tak-šip-an-ni ki-šip-ši
The wicked witch who has cursed me, curse her with the spell [she] used on me!
e-pi-šu i-pu-šá-an-ni ip-šú i-pu-šá-an-ni e-pu-su
The sorcerer who has ensnared me, ensnare him with the spell [he] used on me!
e-piš-tu te-pu-šá-an-ni ip-šú te-pu-šá-an-ni e-pu-si
The sorceress who has ensnared me, ensnare her with the spell [she] used on me!

[130] muš-te-piš-tu te-pu-šá-an-ni ip-šú te-pu-šá-an-ni e-pu-si
The enchantress who bewitched me; now bewitch her with the spell [she] used on me!
šá salmânimeš ana pi-i salmânimeš-ia ib-nu-ú
Who made [images] in my [image] and mimicked my shape;
bu-un-na-an-ni-ia ú-mašši-lu ru'ti-ia il-qu-ú šârti-ia im-lu-su
they drained my saliva, they ripped at my hair,
sissikti-ia ib-tu-qu e-ti-qu epirhi.a šêpê-ia is-bu-su
they cut hems from my robe and steak the earth where my foot falls.
GIRRA qar-du šipat-su-nu li-pa-áš-šir SU.EN
GIRRA [*Fires of God*], undo their incantation!

[135] ÉN anašiši ti-pa-ru salmânimeš-šú-nu a-qal-lu
I raise up the torch that I may burn the figures
šá ú-tuk-ku še-e-du ra-bi-su e-tim-mu
of the Demon, the Spirit, the Lurking Ghost,
la-maš-ti la-ba-si ah-ha-zu
the [*lamastu*], the [*labasu*], the [*ahhazu*],
lúlilu flilitu ardat lili
the [*lilu*], the [*lilitu*], the [*nightmare*],
ù mimma lim-nu mu-sab-bi-tu a-me-lu-ti
and any evil that plagues humanity:

[140] hu-la zu-ba u i-ta-at-tu-ka
dissolve, melt, drip away like wax!
qu-tur-ku-nu li-tel-li šamê
May your smoke drift ever upwards
la-'-mi-ku-nu li-bal-li dšamši
and may the Sun extinguish your coals!
lip-ru-us ha-a-a-ta-ku-nu mâr dé-a maš-mašu SU.EN
May he extinguish your emenations, by the son of ENKI [who is MARDUK], Master of Magicians.

ÉN NUSKU šur-bu-ú ma-lik ilimeš rabû-timeš
(The first line of the next tablet in the series.)
[145] tuppu Ikam ma-aq-lu-ú
(Here ends Tablet I of the MAQLU.)

Tablet II

ÉN NUSKU šur-bu-ú ma-lik ilîmeš rabû-timeš
NUSKU, Might Counselor of the Great Gods!
pa-qid nindabêmeš šá ka-la IGIGI
Overseer of the sacrifices of all IGIGI,
mu-kin ma-ha-zi mu-ud-di-šu parakkêmeš
Founder of cities, who reviews the Seats of Gods!
u-mu nam-ru šá qi-bit-su si-rat
Brilliant shining day, the promise of all goodness,

sukkal da-nim še-mu-ú pi-ris-ti den-lil
Messenger of ANU, obeying the secret of ENLIL,
še-mu-ú den-lil ma-li-ku ša-du-ú IGIGI
Commander ENLIL, counselor of the IGIGI,
gaš-ru ta-ha-zu šá ti-bu-šú dan-nu
Powerful in combat, whose rising is powerful,
NUSKU a-ri-ru mu-šab-riq za-ai-ri
NUSKU, brilliant shinning one who blinds his enemies,
ina ba-li-ka ul iš-šak-kan nap-ta-na ina é-kur
without you there is no meal in the E.KUR,

ina ba-li-ka ilîmeš rabûtimeš ul is-si-nu qut-rin-nu
without you, the Gods do not rise to smell the incense,
ina ba-li-ka SAMAS u ANU ul i-da-a-ni di-i-nu
without you, SAMAS does not hold his court.
ha-sis šu-me-ka te-it-tir ina i-dir-ti ta-ga-mil ina pušqi
Whosoever remembers your name, you deliver [him] from difficulty, sparing [his] miseries.

ana-ku ardu-ka annanna apil annanna šá ilu-šú annanna ISTAR-šú annannitumtum

I am your servant __, son of __, whose god is __ and whose goddess is __.

as-hur-ka eš-e-ka na-šá-a qâtâ-ai šá-pal-ka ak-mis

I turn to you, seek you out, hands raised; I throw myself at your feet:

[15] qu-mi kaš-šá-pi ù kaš-šap-ti

Burn the evil warlock and the wicked witch,

šá lúkaššapi-ia u kaššapti-ia ár-hiš ha-an-tiš napišta-šú-nu lib-li-ma

My warlock and witch, may they lose their life quickly.

ia-a-ši bul-lit-an-ni-ma nar-bi-ka lu-šá-pi dà-li-li-ka lud-lul

Spare my life so I will be forever in your debt, alive to praise your greatness all my days!

INIM-INIM-MA ÚH-BÚR-RU-DA sa-lam lipî-KÉ
(spells to dissolve magic with the help of salt images.)

ÉN GIRRA BELu git-ma-lu gaš-ra-a-ta na-bi šum-ka
GIRRA, "You are powerful" is the meaning of your name.

dnanna-ra-ta na-bi šùm-ka
NANNA, your eyes see all things.
tuš-nam-mar bitatimeš ka-la-ma
Your light brightens dark places, light of the moon over all countries.
tuš-nam-mar gi-im-ra ka-liš ma-ta-a-ti
Your light brightens all things, so I stand before you,
áš-šu at-ta ta-az-za-zu-ma
because you restore divine Justice.
ki-ma NANNA-SIN ù SAMAS ta-din-nu di-i-nu
Like NANNA-SIN & SAMAS you make things right,

di-e-ni di-ni purussâ-a-a purusus
So restore the right in my life, be a judge of my decision.
a-na nûri-ka nam-ri az-ziz
To your brilliant shinning light, I come.
a-na elle-ti ti-pa-ri-ka az-ziz
To the brilliant shinning torch, I come.
BELU sissiktu-ka as-bat
Lord, I grab at the hem of your robe,
sissikat ilu-ti-ka rabi-ti as-bat
the hem of your divine robe I am grabbing.

<unreadable part> -si il-ta-si eli-ia
is-bat lìb-bi qaqqadi kišâdi-ia u muh-hi
[She] attacks the heart, the head, the neck and the face.

is-bat ênê-ia na-ti-la-a-ti
[She] attacks my watchful eyes,
is-bat sêpê-ia al-la-ka-a-ti
attacks my walking feet,
is-bat bir-ki-ia ib-bi-ri-e-ti
attacks my moving knees [joints],

is-bat idê-ia mut-tab-bil-a-ti
attacks my strengthened arms.
e-nin-na ina ma-har ilu-ti-ka rabîtiti
Now I come before your Divine Greatness,
salmânimeš siparri it-gu-ru-ti
[I set before you] the 'crossed' copper [images]
lúkaššapi-ia u kaššapti-ia
of my evil warlock and wicked witch,
e-piš-ia u muš-te-piš-ti-ia
my sorcerer and sorceress,

sa-hir-ia u sa-hir-ti-ia
my stupifier and stupifyress,
ra-hi-ia u ra-hi-ti-ia
my enchanter and enchantress,
BEL ik-ki-ia u BELIT ik-ki-ia
my lord and lady who opposes me,
BEL sir-ri-ia u BELIT sir-ri-ia
my lord and lady who is my enemy,
BEL ri-di-ia u BELIT ri-di-ia
my lord and lady who prosecutes me,

BEL di-ni-ia u BELIT di-ni-ia
my lord and lady who accuses me,
BEL amâti-ia u BELIT amâti-ia
my lord and lady who slanders against me,

BEL dabâbi-ia u BELIT dabâbi-ia
my lord and lady defector,
BEL egirri-ia u BELIT egirri-ia
my lord and lady nemesis,
BEL limuttimtim-ia u BELIT limuttimtim-ia
my lord and lady evil-doers:

ana lúmiti pu-qu-du-in-ni
They gave me over to the dead;
nam-ra-su kul-lu-mu-in-ni
They bound me in their ridicule,
utukku lim-nu lu-u alû lim-nu lu-u etim-mu lim-nu
to the evil [*utukku*] or evil [*alu*] or [*etimmu*],
gallû lim-nu lu-u ilu lim-nu lu-u râbisu lim-nu
the evil [*gallu*] or evil god [*ilu*] or [*rabisu*],
lamaštu lu-u labasu lu-u ahhazu
the evil [*lamastu*] or [*labasu*] or [*ahhazu*]

lúlilu lu-u flilitu lu-u ardat lili
the evil [*lilu*] or [*lilitu*] or [*ardat lili*]
lu-u li-'-bu si-bit šadi
or evil fever, like the [*sibit sadi*] disease,
lu-u be-en-nu ri-hu-ut dšul-pa-è-a
or befallen with epilepsy and seizures,
lu-u AN-TA-ŠUB-BA lu-u DINGIR-HUL
or [*antasubba*] or the "Evil God",
lu-u ŠU-DINGIR-RA lu-u ŠU-IN-NIN-NA
or "Hand of God" or "Hand of Goddess",

lu-u ŠU-GIDIM-MA lu-u ŠU-UDUG
or "hand" of the Spirit of the Dead or of [*utukki*]
lu-u ŠU-NAM-LÚ-LÍL-LU lu-u la-maš-tu sihirtutú marat da-nim
or "hand" of a human or [*lamastu*] Anu's daughter,

lu-u SAG-HUL-HA-ZA mu-kil rêš li-muttim
or [*sagulaza*], the record-keeper of debts,
lu-u di-kis šêrêmeš šim-ma-tú ri-mu-tú
or the roasting of flesh, paralysis, consumption,
lu mimma lim-nu šá šu-ma la na-bu-u
or everything bad that is without names,

lu mimma e-piš li-mut-ti šá a-me-lu-ti
or anything that is baneful to human beings,
šá sab-ta-ni-ma mu-ša u ur-ra iredú-nimeš-ni
that which makes me a prisoner at night, that which chases me during the day,
ú-hat-tu-ú šêrêmeš-ia kal u-mi sab-ta-ni-ma
that which eats my flesh, seizes my body,
kal mu-si la ú-maš-šar-an-ni
which will not give me rest for a single night!
e-nin-na ina ma-har ilu-ti-ka rabîtiti
Now, I come before your Divine Greatness,

ina kibri-dit ellititi a-qal-li-šú-nu-ti a-šar-rap-šú-nu-ti
I burn and incinerate them completely with sulfur.
nap-li-sa-an-ni-ma be-lum ú-suh-šú-nu-ti ina zumri-ia
Look favorably on me, tear them out of my body,
pu-šur kiš-pi-šú-nu lim-nu-ti
disintegrate their evil spell!
at-ta GIRRA be-lum a-li-ki i-di-ia
GIRRA [*fires of God*] be at my side,
bul-lit-an-ni-ma nar-bi-ka lu-šá-pi dà-li-li-ka lud-lul
Keep me alive that I may praise, adore and serve.

INIM-INIM-MA ÚH-BÚR-RU-DA sa-lam siparri kibri-dit-KÉ
(Here continues the incantation to undo a spell with a copper image and sulfur.)

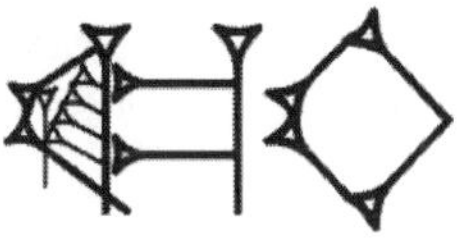

ÉN GIRRA a-ri-ru bu-kur da-nim
GIRRA [*fires of God*] born of ANU,
da-'-in di-ni-ia at-me-e pi-ris-ti at-ta-ma
who guides my hearing and judges my decision;
ik-li-e-ti tu-uš-nam-mar
you bring the darkness to light,
e-šá-a-ti dal-ha-a-ti tu-uš-te-eš-šir
you bring order to the chaos or destroyed;

a-na ilimeš rabûtimeš purussâa ta-nam-din
to the Great Gods you grant resolutions,
šá la ka-a-ta ilu ma-am-man purussâa ul i-par-ra-as
but for you no God makes your decisions.
at-ta-ma na-din ur-ti ù te-e-me
It is for you to give order and directions;
e-piš lum-ni at-ta-ma ar-hiš ta-kam-mu
you alone bind the evil and the evil-doer,
lim-nu ai-bu ta-kaš-šad ar-hiš
you strike down the evil enemy with swiftness.

a-na-ku annanna mar ili-šu šá ilu-šú an-nanna ISTAR-šu annannitum
I am __ , a son of his god, whose god is __ and whose goddess is __.
ina kiš-pi lu-up-pu-ta-ku-ma ma-har-ka az-ziz
I am bewitched, this is why I have come to you!
ina pân ili u šarri na-zu-ra-ku-ma du ana mah-ri-ka
Before God and King I have turned toward you!

elî a-me-ri-ia mar-sa-ku-ma šá-pal-ka ak-mis
Unpleasant to behold, I throw myself before you!
GIRRA šur-bu-ú ilu el-lu
GIRRA – Radiant Fires of God!

e-nin-na ina ma-har ilu-ti-ka rabîtiti
I come before your Divine Greatness,
salmanimeš lúkaššapi u kaššapti šá siparri e-pu-uš qa-tuk-ka
I have made two [images] of the evil warlock and wicked witch, in copper, by your hand:
ma-har-ka ú-gir-šú-nu-ti-ma ka-a-šá ap-kid-ka
In front of you I have 'crossed' them, I give them over to you.
šu-nu li-mu-tu-ma ana-ku lu-ub-lut
Cause them death that I may live!
šu-nu li-ti-ib-bi-ru-ma ana-ku lu-ši-ir
Their paths detract, but I go straight!

šu-nu liq-tu-ú-ma ana-ku lu-um-id
They reach limits, but I continue to grow!
šu-nu li-ni-šu-ma ana-ku lu-ud-nin
They become weak, but I continue to be strong!
GIRRA šar-hu si-ru šá ilimeš
GIRRA, brilliant flame among the gods,
ka-šid lim-ni u ai-bi kušus-su-nu-ti-ma a-na-ku la ah-hab-bil
you seize the evil and evil-doer; seize them so I may not be destroyed,
ana-ku ardu-ka lul-ub-lut lu-uš-lim-ma ma-har-ka lu-uz-ziz
I, your servant, may remain living safe, able to stand in front of you!

at-ta-ma ili-ia at-ta-ma be-li
You are my god, my lord supreme,
at-ta-ma da-ai-ni at-ta-ma ri-su-ú-a
You are my judge, my divine assistance,
at-ta-ma mu-tir-ru šá gi-mil-li-ia TU.EN
You are my avenger, avenge me!

INIM-INIM-MA ÚH-BÚR-RU-DA sa-lam siparri-KÉ
(*An incantation to remove a spell using a bronze image.*)

ÉN GIRRA a-ri-ru mar da-nim qar-du
GIRRA [*fires of God*] born of ANU!

iz-zu ahemeš-šú at-ta
Straightforward among your brethren;
šá ki-ma NANNA-SIN u SAMAS ta-da-an-nu di-i-nu
Like NANNA-SIN and SAMAS you make things right.
di-i-ni di-ni purussâ-ai purusus
Grant me justice, be the judge of my decision.
qu-mi kaš-šá-pi ù kaš-šap-ti
Burn the evil warlock and wicked witch!
GIRRA qu-mu lúkaššapi u kaššapti
GIRRA, burn the warlock and witch!

GIRRA qu-li lúkaššapi u kaššapti
GIRRA, boil the warlock and witch!
GIRRA qu-mi-šú-nu-ti
GIRRA, incinerate them to nothing!

GIRRA qu-li-šú-nu-ti
GIRRA, boil them down!
GIRRA ku-šu-us-su-nu-ti
GIRRA, seize them!
GIRRA a-ru-uh-šú-nu-ti
GIRRA, devour them!

[115] GIRRA su-ta-bil-šú-nu-ti
GIRRA, remove them!
e-piš kiš-pi lim-nu-ti u ru-hi-e la tabûtimeš
They who inflict evil and the baneful spell,
šá a-na li-mut-ti ik-pu-du-ni ia-a-ši
Who think upon me with evil intention:
dan-nu ma-ak-kur-šu-nu šu-ul-qi
Let a criminal steal their possessions!
šu-bil bu-šá-šu-nu ik-ki-e-ma
Let a thief make off with their property!

[120] elî ma-na-ha-te-šu-nu hab-ba-ta šur-bi-is
Let a burglar invade their home!
GIRRA iz-zu git-ma-lu ra-šub-bu
GIRRA, wrathful, perfect and all-powerful
ina é-kur a-šar tal-lak-ti-ka tu-šap-šah-šu-nu-ti a-di sur-riš
In E.KUR, when you return, you will find peace!
ina a-mat dé-a ba-ni-ka ù SAMAS an-nam-ru
By the incandation of ENKI, your progenitor and of SAMAS, I have become radiant;
apqallê šuut eri-du lik-pi-du-šú-nu-ti ana limnuttimtim SU.EN
May the seven [*apkallu*] of ERIDU look onto them with evil intention!

[125] INIM-INIM-MA ÚH-BÚR-RU-DA sa-lam liši-KÉ
(*An incantation to remove a spell with a dough image.*)

ÉN GIRRA gaš-ru u-mu na-an-du-ru
GIRRA, commanding force of terrible weather!
tuš-te-eš-šir ilimeš u ma-al-ki
You lead the gods and peoples rightfully!
ta-da-a-ni di-ÉN hab-li u ha-bil-ti
You lead the trials of the oppressed peoples;
ina di-ni-ia i-ziz-za-am-ma ki-ma SAMAS qu-ra-du
be also present at my trial! Like SAMAS,

[130] di-i-ni di-ni purussâ-ai purusus
lead my trial and be judge of my decision.
qu-mi kaš-ša-pi u kaš-šap-ti
Burn the evil warlock and wicked witch!
a-kul ai-bi-ia a-ru-uh lim-nu-ti-ia
Devour my enemies, those who wish me evil!
ûm-ka iz-zu lik-šu-us-su-nu-ti NANNA-SIN
May they be caught up in your terrible weather!

INIM-INIM-MA ÚH-BÚR-RU-DA sa-lam titi-KÉ
(An incantation to reverse a spell with a bronze image.)

ÉN GIRRA šar-hu bu-kur da-nim
GIRRA [*fires of God*] born of ANU!
i-lit-ti ellitimtim šá-qu-tum dša-la-aš
Radiant ray of the Great [*salas*]!
šar-hu id-di-šu-u zik-ri ilimeš ka-ai-nu
Divine, ever-renewing, constant, Word of the Gods,
na-din nin-da-bi-e ana ilimeš IGIGI
who distributes the offerings to the gods [*IGIGI*],
šá-kin na-mir-ti a-na da-nun-na-ki ilimeš rabûtimeš
who gives radiance to the ANUNNAKI – the Great Gods!

iz-zu GIRRA muš-har-mit a-pi
Raging GIRRA, who destroys the pathway,
GIRRA al-la-lu-ú mu-ab-bit isemeš u ab-nemeš
GIRRA, strength to destroy wood and stone,
qa-mu-ú lim-nu-ti zêr lúkaššapi u kaš-šapti
who burns the evil seed of the warlock and witch,
mu-hal-liq rag-gi zêr lúkaššapi u kaš-šapti
who incinerates the wicked seed of the warlock and witch!
ina u-mi an-ni-i ina di-ni-ia i-ziz-za-am-ma
Come to my trial this day, come raging!

e-piš bar-ti te-na-na-a ku-šu-ud lim-nu
Maker of submission, who seizes all that is evil!
kima salmânimeš an-nu-ti i-hu-lu i-zu-bu u it-ta-at-tu-ku
Like these figures drip away, melting and dissolving away,

ki-ma šu-šu-rat bîti ana bâbi ana na-sa-ki-ia
Like garbage they have tried to discard of me!
ana-ku ina qi-bit MARDUK u BEL nu-bat-ti
I speak the incantation of MARDUK, Lord of the Night

u dasari-lú-du BEL a-ši-pu-ti
MARDUK [*asariludu*], the Master of Magic[ians],
e-pi-šu u e-piš-ti
the evil sorcerer and sorceress;
ki-ma ki-i-ti a-kap-pil-šu-nu-ti
like a ball of wool, I will roll them!
ki-ma hu-ha-ri a-sa-hap-šu-nu-ti
Like a bird-clapper, I take them down!
ki-ma ka-a-pi ab-ba-šu-nu-ti
Like a mason-stone, I destroy them!

ki-ma še-e-ti a-kat-tam-šu-nu-ti
Like a net, I ensnare them!
ki-ma pi-til-ti a-pat-til-šu-nu-ti
Like a candlewick, I snuff them out!
ki-ma pi-ti-iq-ti ab-ba-lak-kit-šu-nu-ti
Like a cliff-wall, I climb over them!
ki-ma mêmeš mu-sa-a-ti a-sur-ra-a ú-ma-al-la-šú-nu-ti
With unclean waters I fill them up!
ki-ma šu-šu-rat bîti ana bâbi a-na-as-sik-šú-nu-ti
Like garbage, I discard them!

titalliš lil-li-ka salam lúkaššapi u kaššapti ÉN
May the [image] of the evil warlock and wicked witch be burned to ash!

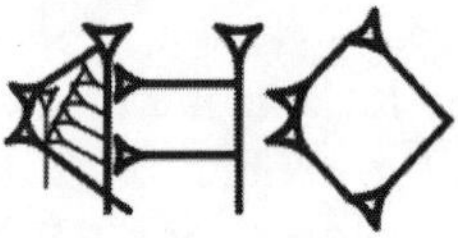

INIM-INIM-MA ÚH-BÚR-RU-DA sa-lam ittî šá gassa bullulu-KÉ
(*An incantation to reverse a spell using a plaster image.*)

ÉN at-ti man-nu kassaptušá ina nâri im-lu-' tita-ai
What is your name, witch? Who are you, who made an [image] of me from river-clay?
ina bîti e-ti-i ú-tam-me-ru salmanimeš-ia
Who burned my [image] in her dark house?
ina qab-rì it-mi-ru mu-ú-a
Who has spilled my water over a grave?

ina tub-qi-na-ti ú-laq-qí-tu hu-sa-bi-e-a
Who has stolen sprigs of my fruit trees?
ina bit lúašlaki ib-tu-qu sissikti-ia
Who has cut seams of my robe?
ina askuppati iš-bu-šu epirhi.a šêpê-ia
Who has gathered up the earth beneath my feet?
áš-pur ana bâb ka-a-ri i-šá-mu-ú-ni li-pa-a-ki
I send to the harbor where you buy salt;
áš-pur ana hi-rit ali iq-ri-su-ú-ni ti-i-ta-ki
I send to the beach where you gather clay;

áš-ta-pa-rak-kim-ma a-li-ku ti-nu-ru
I send you a furnace for your operations,
GIRRA mu-un-na-ah-zu
with GIRRA [*fires of God*] already lit,
GIRRA id-di-šu-u nur ilimeš ka-ai-nu
GIRRA [*fires of God*], constant light of the gods;

NANNA-SIN ina uruki SAMAS ina larsaki
NANNA-SIN in Ur, SAMAS in Larsa,
NERGAL a-di um-ma-na-ti-šú
NERGAL waiting next to his people,

ISTAR a-ga-deki a-di ku-um-mi-šá
INANNA-ISHTAR in Akkad next to her house:
a-na la-qa-at zêri lúkaššapi u kaššapti
may they seize the seed of the evil warlock and wicked witch,
ma-la ba-šu-ú
no matter how numerous they may be,
kaššapta li-du-ku-ma ana-ku lu-ub-lut
may they kill the witch that I may remain alive!
áš-šu la e-pu-šá-áš-šim-ma i-pu-šá
I did not bewitch her, she bewitched me!

áš-šu la as-hu-ra-áš-šim-ma is-hu-ra
I did not enchant her, she enchanted me!
ši-i tak-lat ana kiš-pi šá kit-pu-du-ú-ti
She believes in the spell she designed,
ù a-na-ku a-na ez-zu GIBIL da-a-a-nu
but I put my trust in GIBIL to be my judge!
GIRRA qu-mi-ši GIRRA qu-li-ši
GIRRA, burn [her], GIRRA incinerate [her]!
GIRRA šu-ta-bil-ši TU.EN
GIRRA, strike [her] down!

[205] INIM-INIM-MA ÚH-BÚR-RU-DA sa-lam titi šá lipâ bullulu-ké
(An incantation using a clay image dusted in talcum.)

ÉN at-ti man-nu kaššaptu šá tub-ta-na-in-ni
What is your name, witch? You who unceasingly pays me visits?
a-na li-mut-ti taš-te-ni-'-in-ni
Who looks for me with baneful intentions?
a-na la ta-ab-ti ta-as-sa-na-ah-hur-in-ni
Who looks for me with malicious intent?
al-ki ul i-di bit-ki ul i-di šum-ki ul i-di šu-bat-ki ul i-di
I don't know your city, your house or your name.

[210] dšêdêmeš li-ba-'-ki
May the sedu [daemons] visit you,
utukkêmeš liš-te-'-u-ki
May the utukku [daemons] seek you out,
etimmêmeš lis-sah-ru-ú-ki
May the ghosts of the dead haunt you,
be-en-nu la ta-a-bu eli-ki lim-qut
May epilepsy seize you!
rabisêmeš li-mut-ti li-kil-lu rêš-ki
May the evil seat decapitate you!

[215] <unreadable text> dšul-pa-è-a li-na-ru-ki
<unreadable text> -ki li-ip-šit
GIBIL iz-zu la pa-du-u lìb-bi-ki lí-is-su-uh
GIBIL, furious, without pity, smite thee!
dgu-la a-zu-gal-la-tu rabitutu li-it-ki li-im-has
GULA, mighty physician, strike thee down!
GIBIL iz-zu zu-mur-ki li-ih-mut
GIBIL, furious, consume and burn your body!

ellitumtum mârat da-nim šá šamê
Pure daughter of the Sky-God ANU,
šá ina kar-pat na-an-hu-za-at is-atu
who spreads herself in the Divine Vessel
libbi GIBIL qar-du sa-ma-a
bound with the hear of GIBIL, mighty hero...
<unreadable text> šá-ma-mi ik-šu-du
<unreadable text> qu-li i kat-ta <unreadable text>

qu-mi ha-an-tiš šá lúkaššapi-ia u kaššapti-ia
incinerate quickly my evil warlock and wicked witch,
na-piš-ta-šú-nu lib-li-ma
uproot their existence!
ia-a-ši bul-lit-an-ni-ma nar-bi-ka lu-šá-pi
Allow me to live so that I may praise, honor and
dà-li-li-ka lud-lul SU.EN
adore your name!

INIM-INIM-MA ÚH-BÚR-ru-da sa-lam isbini salam iserini-KÉ
(*An incantation to reverse a spell using a wooden image.*)

ÉN kaššaptu mut-tal-lik-tum šá sûqâ-timeš
(*The first line of the next tablet in the series.*)

tuppu IIkam ma-aq-lu-ú
(*Here ends the second tablet of the MAQLU.*)

Tablet III

ÉN kassaptumut-tal-lik-tú šá sûqâtimeš
The [witch] who travels on the roads,
mu-tir-rib-tum šá bîtâtimeš
who invades the people's houses,
da-ai-li-tum šá bi-ri-e-ti
who walks in the alleyways,
sa-ai-di-tum šá ri-ba-a-ti
who hunts in the public district;

a-na pani-šá ù arki-šá is-sa-na-ah-hur
she turns about, showing front and back,
izzazaz ina sûqi-ma ú-sah-har šêpê
she stays in place while still moving her feet,
i-na ri-bi-ti ip-ta-ra-as a-lak-tú
in the public district, she blocks the way.
šá etli damqi du-us-su i-kim
She steals the strength of the innocent man.
šá ardatu damiqtumtum i-ni-ib-šá it-bal
She steals the fruit of the innocent girl,

i-na ni-kil-mi-šá ku-zu-ub-šá il-qi
and with one look, she takes away beauty,
etla ip-pa-lis-ma dûta-šu i-kim
she sees a man and takes his strength,
ardata ip-pa-lis-ma i-ni-ib-šá it-bal
she sees a girl and takes her beauty.
i-mu-ra-an-ni-ma kassaptuil-li-ka arki-ia
The witch saw me and followed,
i-na im-ti-šá ip-ta-ra-as a-lak-tú
and with her venom she has disrupted my way,

i-na ru-hi-šá iš-di-hi ip-ru-us
with magick she has hindered my stride.
ú-šá-as-si ili-ia u ISTAR-ia ina zumri-ia
She takes me away from my god and my goddess.
šá kaššapti ina kul-la-ti aq-ta-ri-is tîta-šá
For the [image] of the witch I have used clay,
šá e-piš-ti-ia ab-ta-ni salam-šá
an [image] of the sorceress I have made.
áš-kun i-na lìb-bi-ki lipû ha-bil-ki
In your body I place [*talcum*], the destroyer of all.

ú-sa-an-niš ina kalatimeš-ki e-ra qa-ma-ki
In your body I put wood to burn you with,
e-ra qa-ma-ki a-mat-ki lip-ru-us
the wood that burns and stops your venom!
e-li âli at-ta-pah i-šá-ti
Above the city, I kindle a fire;
ina šaplan âli at-ta-di lik-ti
beneath the city, I sprinkle a potion.
a-na bît ter-ru-ba at-ta-di i-šá-ti
Wherever you go, I set it on fire.

te-pu-šim-ma GIBIL li-kul-ki
When you show yourself, GIBIL devours you!
tu-še-pi-šim-ma GIBIL lik-šu-ud-ki
When you rest yourself, GIBIL seizes you!
tak-pu-di-ma GIBIL li-duk-ki
When you move about, may GIBIL kill you!
tu-šak-pi-di-ma GIBIL lik-me-ki
When you breathe, may GIBIL burn you!
har-ra-an la ta-ri li-šá-as-bit-ki GIBIL ha-bil-ki
To the 'Land of No Return' may GIBIL bring you!

[30] GIBIL ez-zu zumur-ki li-ih-mut SU.EN
GIBIL, raging force, burns your existence!

ÉN-ta ši-na mârâtimeš da-nim šá šamêe
Two daughters of the Sky-God ANU,
ši-na mârâtimeš da-nim šá šamêe
Three daughters of the Sky-God ANU!
tur-ri ul-ta-nim-ma ul-tu šamêe ur-ra-da-ni
The descend from a ladder, from the sky!
e-ka-a-ma te-ba-ti-na e-ki-a-am tal-la-ka
When do you ascend? Where do you go?

[35] a-na e-pi-ši u e-piš-ti šá annanna apil annanna
The sorcerer and sorceress of __ son of __ ?
ana sahari ni-il-li-ka
We went to cast a spell,
a-na lu-uq-qu-ti šá hu-sa-bi-ši-na
We went to gather sprigs of their fruit-trees,
a-na hu-um-mu-mi šá hu-ma-ma-ti-ši-na
We went to gather up their garbage,
šá li-la-a-ti hu-lu-pa-qa a-na ša-ra-pi ni-il-li-ka
We went in the night to burn the *huluppu*-ship!

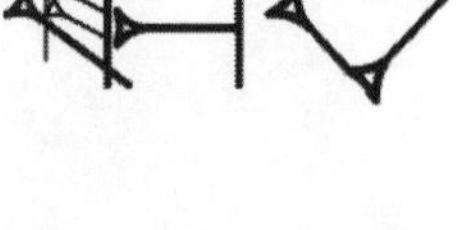

ÉN kassaptunir-ta-ni-tum
Sorceress. Murderess.
e-li-ni-tum nar-šin-da-tum
Nightmare. [*narsindatu*].
a-ši-ip-tum eš-še-pu-ti
[*aspitu*]. Priestess of the Magick Arts.
mušlahhatumtum a-gu-gi-il-tum
Snake-Charmer. [*agugiltu*].
qadištu naditu
Prostitute. [*naditu*].

ISTAR-i-tum zêr-ma-ši-tum
ISHTAR-devotee, [*zermasitu*],
ba-ai-r-tum šá mu-ši
who captures the night,
sa-ayyu-di-tum šá kal u-mi
who hunts the whole of the day,
mu-la-'-i-tum šá šamêe
who putrefies the skies,
mu-lap-pit-tum šá irsitimtim
and touches down on earth,

ka-mi-tum šá pî ilimeš
distorting the mouths of the gods,
ka-si-tum šá bir-ki ISTAR-âtimeš
binding up the knees of the goddesses,
da-ai-ik-tum šá etlêmeš
who kills the people's men,
la pa-di-tum šá dsin-nišâtimeš
who doesn't spare the women,
šá-ah-hu-ti-tum sab-bu-ri-tu
You are a destroyer – an evil woman!

[55] šá ana ip-ši-šá u ru-hi-šá la u-šar-ru man-ma
Against your sorceries and witchcraft none fight!
e-nin-na-ma e-tam-ru-ki is-sab-tu-ki
Now they see you – and they grab you,
uš-te-nu-ki uš-ta-bal-ki-tu-ki
they change you, they bring you to instability,
uš-ta-pi-lu a-mat ip-ši-ki
they have mixed up your magick word,
dé-a u MARDUK id-di-nu-ki ana GIRRA qu-ra-di
ENKI and MARDUK; they cast you to GIRRA!

[60] GIRRA qu-ra-du ri-kis-ki li-ih-pi
GIRRA, may he burn your knots,
ù mimma ma-la te-pu-ši li-šam-hir-ki ka-a-ši
and every sorcery you spoke falls back on you!

ÉN dit el-lu nam-ru qud-du-šu ana-ku
I am the Light! A pure river, shinning, I am!
e-pi-šu-u-a apqallu šá apsî
My sorcerer is the wise one of the deep.
e-pi-še-tu-ú-a mârâtimeš da-nim šá šamêe
My sorceress are the daughters of the Sky-God, ANU.

e-pu-šu-u-ni e-te-ni-ip-pu-šu-u-ni
They speak sorcery onto me unceasingly,
e-pu-šu-nim-ma ul ip-du-u zu-um-ri
they have bewitched and spared me nothing;
e-te-ni-pu-šu-nim-ma ul i-li-'-ú sa-ba-ti-ia
they endless work magick but cannot seize me!
a-na-ku e-pu-uš-ma pi-šu-nu as-bat
I have magick! And I catch their words in my hand!
e-te-bi-ib kima dit ina šadi-ia
I have become brilliantly shinning like the rivers
[*euphrates* and *tigris*] in my land.

e-te-lil ki-ma nam-ru ana bît purussî-ia
I have become pure as the Shinning One.
šá lúkaššapi-ia u kaššapti-ia
My evil warlock and wicked witch,
dit-ru na-bal-kat-ta-šú-nu lis-ku-nu-ma
the river, may it swallow them!
kiš-pu-šu-nu elî-šu-nu li-bal-ki-tu-ma
May their deceit come back on them,
a-na muh-hi-šu-nu u la-ni-šu-nu lil-li-ku
and fall upon them as dust on this [image]!

ki-ma di-iq-me-en-ni li-is-li-mu pa-ni-šú-nu
May their burned face be blackened with ash!
li-hu-lu li-zu-bu u lit-ta-at-tu-ku
May they drip [like wax], melt away and dissolve,
u ana-ku ki-ma dit ina šadî-ia lû ellêkuku SU.ÉN
but I, like the river, remain pure!

ÉN la-man-ni su-tu-ú e-la-mu-ú ri-da-an-ni
The SUTI-tribe surrounds me, I am chased by the Elamites!
kat-man-ni a-gu-ú e-du-ú sah-panan-ni
I am surrounded by floodwater and raging storms!

kassaptusu-ta-ta da-a-nu i-bit-su
The witch is of the SUTI-tribe, her attack fails!
e-le-ni-tu e-la-ma-ta li-pit-sa mu-ú-tu
The nightmare is an Elamite whose hit means death!
GIBIL tap-pi-e SAMAS i-ziz-za-am-ma
GIBIL, friend of SAMAS, come forth unto me!
ki-ma šadi ina kibri-dit i-nu-uh-hu
Like the mountain comes to rest in sulfur,
kiš-pi ru-hi-e ru-si-e šá kaššapti-ia
so may the sorceress and witches, the magick spell of my evil-doers

e-li-ni-ti-ia GIBIL liq-mi
and of my nightmares, may GIBIL burn them all!
dit ellu lib-ba-šá li-ih-pi
May the 'Pure River' break her heart!
mêmeš ellûtimeš lip-šu-ra kiš-pi-šá
May the 'Pure Water' dissolve her spell,
u ana-ku ki-ma dit ina šadî-ia lu ellêkuku SU.ÉN
and I, like the river, remain pure!

ÉN at-ti nam-nu kassaptušá bašûu
What is your name, witch?

a-mat limuttimtim-ia ina lib-bi-šá
Whose heart possesses the baneful word,
ina lišâni-šá ib-ba-nu-ú ru-hu-ú-a
on whose tongue the baneful magick forms,
ina šap-ti-šá ib-ba-nu-ú ru-su-ú-a
on whose lips the spell against me starts?
i-na ki-bi-is tak-bu-us izzazaz mu-ú-tum
In your footsteps stands death.
kassaptuas-bat pi-ki as-bat lišân-ki
Wicked Witch, I seize your words [tongue/mouth],

as-bat ênê-ki na-ti-la-a-ti
I seize your eyes,
as-bat šêpê-ki al-la-ka-a-ti
I seize your feet,
as-bat bir-ki-ki e-bi-ri-e-ti
I seize your legs,
as-bat idê-ki mut-tab-bi-la-a-ti
I seize your right arm,
ak-ta-si i-di-ki a-na ar-ki-ki
then tie both arms behind your back!

NANNA-SIN el-lam-mi-e li-qat-ta-a pagar-ki
May NANNA-SIN, twin-form, destroy your body,
a-na mi-qit mêmeš u išâti lid-di-ki-ma
cast you in a ditch of water of fire!
kassaptuki-ma si-hir kunukki an-ni-e
[Witch], like the interior of the furnace,
li-su-du li-ri-qu pa-nu-ú-ki
may your face become burnt yellow!

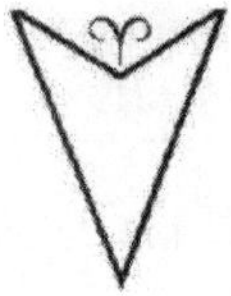

ÉN at-ti e šá te-pu-ši-in-ni
You have betwitched me!

at-ti e šá tu-še-pi-ši-in-ni
You have charmed me!
at-ti e šá tu-kaš-ši-pi-in-ni
You have enchanted me!
at-ti e šá tu-hap-pi-pi-in-ni
You have oppressed me!
at-ti e šá tu-sab-bi-ti-in-ni
You have seized me!
at-ti e šá tu-kan-ni-ki-in-ni
You have suffocated me!

at-ti e šá tu-ab-bi-ti-in-ni
You have destroyed me!
at-ti e šá tu-ub-bi-ri-in-ni
You have tied me!
at-ti e šá tu-ka-si-in-ni
You have bound me!
at-ti e šá tu-la-'-in-ni
You have confounded me!
tap-ru-si itti-ia ili-ia u ISTAR-ia
You have kept my God and Goddess from me,

tap-ru-si itti-ia še-' še-tu ahu ahattu ib-ru tap-pu u ki-na-at-tu
kept away my friend, consort, brother, sister and family, companions and servants!

a-liq-qa-kim-ma ha-ha-a šá utuni um-mi-nu šá diqâri
I scrape flakes of ash from the oven and soot from the pots,
a-mah-ha-ah a-tab-bak ana qaqqad rag-ga-ti šim-ti-ki
I mix them with water and it drips over the head of your evil [image] figure.

ÉN šá e-pu-šá-ni uš-te-pi-šá-an-ni
Who has bewitched me? Who has enchanted me?
i-na mi-li nâri e-pu-šá-an-ni
In the river high waters, who has bewitched me?

i-na mi-ti nari e-pu-šá-an-ni
In the river low waters, who has bewitched me?
a-na e-piš-ti ip-ši-ma iq-bu-ú
Who said to the sorceress, "Cast your sorcery"?
a-na sa-hir-ti suh-ri-ma iq-bu-ú
Who said to the inspired, "Make him insane"?
an-ni-tu lu-u maqurru-šá
This is her boat.
kima maqurru an-ni-tu ib-ba-lak-ki-tu
Like the boat crosses back across the waters,

kis-pu-šá lib-bal-ki-tu-ma ina muh-hi-šá
so too may her spells come back and cross on her head
u la-ni-šá lil-li-ku
and her figure [body]! So be it!

di-in-šá lis-sa-hi-ip-ma di-e-ni li-šir SU.ÉN
May [she] be defeated while I remain victorious!

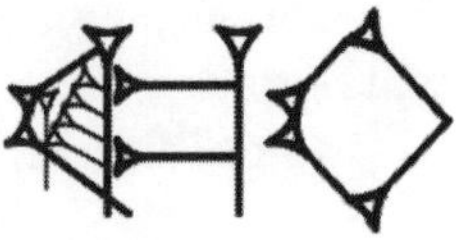

ÉN maqurri-ia a-na NANNA-SIN ú-še-piš
My boat is built by NANNA-SIN,
ina bi-rit qârnemeš-šá na-šat pi-šir-tum
between the horns stands the potion as cargo;

[130] áš-bu ina lìb-bi-šá lúkaššapu u kaššaptu
inside it, the evil warlock and wicked witch sit;
áš-bu ina lìb-bi-šá e-piš u e-piš-tú
inside it, the sorcerer and sorceress sit;
áš-bu ina lib-bi-šá sa-hi-ru u sa-hir-tú
inside it, the inspirers of insanity sit.
šá maqurri-ši-na lib-ba-ti-iq a-šá-al-šá
Come, let the the dock-rope by cut!
mar-kas-sa-ši-na lip-pa-tir-ma tar-kul-la-šá
Come, let the moor be loosened from the boat!

[135] a-na qabal tam-ti liq-qil-pu LU <unreadable text>
May it be lost in the midst of the sea!
e-du-u dan-nu a-na tam-tim li-še-si-šú-nu-ti
May a strong wave pull it into the ocean!
šam-ru-ti a-gu-u e-li-šú-nu li-tel-lu-u
May the waves of the sea overpower it!
šar-šú-nu a-a i-zi-qa-am-ma a-a i-hi-ta-a-ni
May a favorable wind not blow, not be had!
ina qi-bit NUSKU u dgirru ilimeš dini-šú-nu ÉN
By the order of NUSKU and GIRRA, the god-judges.

[140] ÉN LA-tú šá su-qa-ti am-me-ni tug-da-nar-ri-ÉN-ni
LATU, why do you pursue me in the street without ceasing?
am-me-ni na-áš-pa-tu-ki it-ta-na-lak-a-ni
Why send your messsages to my head?
kassaptuSAG.DUmeš a-ma-ti-ki
Witch, 'inhibited' is your new word!
am-me-ni it-ta-nak-šá-da a-na lu-<unreadable text>
el-li a-na ú-ri ab-ta-ki a-<unreadable text>
I climb to the heights and see you!

[145] ú-rad a-na qaq-qa-ri-im-ma ú-sab-bi-tu
I climb down to earth and I see you!
ina kib-si-ki râbisa ú-še-šab
On your path, I set the BAN none may pass!
etim ri-da-a-ti harran-ki ú-šá-as-bit
On your path, Iset the dead-spirit of persecution.
a-mah-ha-as muh-ha-ki ú-šá-an-na tè-en-ki
I strike at your head and confuse your mind,
a-dal-lah lìb-ba-ki ta-maš-ši-i šêrêmeš-ki
I bright your spirit to ruin, that you may forget your body,

[150] e-piš-tum u muš-te-piš-tum
sorcerer and sorceress of the deep!
šamûu a-na-ku ul tu-lap-pa-tin-ni
The sky, I am, and you cannot touch me.
irsitumtum a-na-ku ul tu-ra-hi-in-ni
The earth, I am, and you cannot confound me.
si-hi-il isbal-ti a-na-ku ul tu-kab-ba-si-in-ni
The thorn, I am, and you cannot crush me.
zi-qit aqrabi a-na-ku ul tu-lap-pa-tin-ni
The scorpion's sting, I am, you cannot touch me!

[155] šadúu zaq-ru a-na-ku kiš-pi-ki ru-hi-ki
The mountain peak, I am, and your sorceries and enchantment,
ru-su-ú-ki up-šá-šu-ki limnûtimeš
your spell, your evil manifestations,
la itehûmeš-ni la i-qar-ri-bu-u-ni ai-ši SU.ÉN
cannot come close to me, you shall not pass!

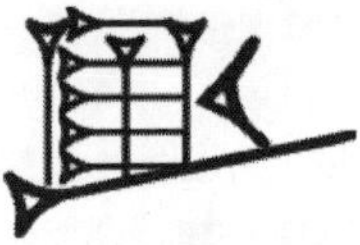

ÉN rit-tu-ma rit-tu
Hand. Hand,
rit-tu dan-na-tu šá a-me-lu-ti
Hand, powerful of men,

[160] šá kîma nêši is-ba-tu a-me-lu
and like a lion, tackles the man,
kima hu-ha-ri is-hu-pu it-lu
like a sling-shot, thrusts the man out to the ground,

kima še-e-ti ú-kat-ti-mu qar-ra-du
like a net, has ensnared the strong [man],
kima šu-uš-kal-li a-šá-rid-du i-bar-ru
like a grappling, has ensnared the leader,
kima giš-par-ri ik-tu-mu dan-na
like a perfect trap, it has caught the most powerful!

[165] lúkaššapu u kassapturit-ta-ku-nu GIRRA liq-mi
The evil warlock and wicked witch, may GIRRA burn your hands,
GIRRA li-kul GIRRA liš-ti GIRRA liš-ta-bil
GIRRA, devour. GIRRA, drink. GIRRA, destroy!
GIRRA lil-sa-a elî dan-na-ti rit-te-ku-nu
GIRRA, scream out against [their] powerful hands!
šá rit-ta-ku-nu e-pu-šu zu-mur-ku-nu li-ih-mut
Your hands are betwitched now, may [GIRRA] burn the whole of your body now!
li-is-pu-uh illat-ku-nu mâr dé-a mašmašu
May the son of ENKI, [MARDUK], Master of the Magicians, destroy your power!

[170] qut-ri GIRRA li-ri-ma pa-ni-ku-nu
Breath of GIRRA, blow against your face!
ki-ma ti-nu-ri ina hi-ta-ti-ku-nu
Like a furnace seeping through its defection,
ki-ma di-qa-ri ina lu-hu-um-me-ku-nu
Like a pot developing its soot,
li-is-pu-uh-ku-nu-ši GIRRA iz-zu
May the raging GIRRA consume and destroy you!
ai ithumeš-ni kiš-pi-ku-nu ru-hi-ku-nu lim-nu-ti
Your witchcraft, your evil spell, shall not come close to me!

e-til-la-a kima nûnêhi.a ina mêmeš-e-a
Climb like a fish in my own water,
kîma šahi ina ru-šum-ti-ia
Like a pig in my sty,
kîma šam-maštakal ina ú-sal-li
Like a seed [*mastakal*] from my meadows,
kîma šam-sassati ina a-hi a-tap-pi
Like the grass [reed] on the riverbanks,
kîma zêr isuši ina a-hi tam-tim
Like the seed of the black tree on the shore!

el-lit ISTAR mu-nam-me-rat šim-ti
Radiant shinning ISHTAR, who brightens the night,
ú-su-rat balati us-su-ra-ku ana-ku
over to whose fate I have been delivered,
ina qi-bit iq-bu-ú GIRRA ra-šub-bu
By the decree of the raging GIRRA [has spoken],
ù GIRRA a-ri-ru mâr da-nim qar-du
and GIRRA the consuming, born of ANU

ÉN rit-tum-ma rit-tum
Hand. Hand,
rit-tum dan-na-tum šá a-me-lu-ti
Hand, powerful of men,

kassaptuáš-šú pi-i-ki da-ab-bi-bu
Witch, because of your strong slander [mouth]
áš-šú dan-na-ti rit-ta-ki
because of your powerful [hand],
álu a-ma-tum áš-šak-ki
I have brought you the Word from the city,
bitu a-ma-tum ú-ba-a-ki
from the [secret] house, I seek the [secret] Word for you.

[190] lúkaššapu u kassaptue-piš u e-piš-tú
Evil warlock and wicked witch; sorcerer and sorceress,
bi-il rit-ta-ku-nu-ma ana išâti lud-di ÉN
I pull down your lifted hand and cast it into the fire!

ÉN biš-li biš-li qi-di-e qi-di-e
(*The first line of the next tablet in the series.*)

tuppu kam ma-aq-lu-ú
(*Here ends the third tablet of the MAQLU.*)

Tablet IV

ÉN biš-li biš-li qi-di-e qi-di-e
Boil, boil, burn, burn!
rag-gu u si-e-nu e te-ru-ub at-lak
Discord and evil, do not enter, keep away!
at-ta man-nu mâr man-ni at-ti man-nu mârat man-ni
Who are you? Born of? Whose son? Whose daughter?

šá áš-ba-tu-nu-ma ip-še-ku-nu up-šá-še-ku-nu
You who sit here and plot your sorcery

te-te-ni-ip-pu-šá-ni ia-a-ši
against me!
lip-šur dé-a mašmašu
May ENKI the Magician
lis-bal-kit kiš-pi-ku-nu
undo and reverse your spells!
dasari-lú-du mašmaš ilimeš mâr dé-a apqallu
MARDUK [*asariludu*], Magician of the Gods, son of ENKI, wise father!
a-kas-si-ku-nu-ši a-kam-mi-ku-nu-ši a-nam-din-ku-nu-ši
I bind you! I tie you up! I give you over

a-na GIRRA qa-mi-e qa-li-i ka-si-i
to GIRRA, burning, incinerating, consuming,
ka-ši-du šá kaššapâtimeš
overpowering and seizing the sorcer[ess]!
GIRRA qa-mu-ú li-tal-lal i-da-ai
GIRRA, incinerating power, give strength to my arms!
ip-šú bar-tu a-mat limuttim râmu zêru
Magick. Revolt. Baneful. Love. Hate.
dipalâa zitarrutâa kadibbidâ KUŠ.HUNGA
Chaos. Murder. Deceit [disease of the mouth].

šabalbalâa su-ud pa-ni u šá-ni-e tè-e-mu
Tearing from the insides. A face turned to insanity.
te-pu-šá-ni tu-še-pi-šá-ni GIRRA lip-šur
What you have done, what you have made others do for you, may GIRRA reverse it!

a-na lúpagri ta-hi-ra-in-ni te-pu-šá-ni tu-še-pi-šá-ni GIRRA lip-šur

You have marked me for dead, may GIRRA undo this!

a-na gul-gul-la-ti tap-qí-da-in-ni te-pu-šá-ni tu-še-pi-šá-ni GIRRA lipšur

You have turned me over to the dead, may GIRRA undo this!

a-na etim kim-ti-ia tap-qí-da-in-ni te-pu-šá-ni tu-še-pi-šá-ni GIRRA lipšur

You have delivered me to the spirits of the dead, may GIRRA undo this!

[20] a-na etim a-hi-i tap-qí-da-in-ni te-pu-šá-ni tu-še-pi-šá-ni GIRRA lip-šur

You have delivered me to the spirits of the unknown dead, may GIRRA undo this!

a-na etimmi mur-tappi-du šá pa-qí-da la i-šu-u te-pu-šá-ni tu-še-pi-šá-ni-GIRRA lip- šur

You have given me to a wandering spirit, may GIRRA undo this!

a-na etim har-bi na-du-ti tap-qí-da-in-ni te-pu-šá-ni tu-še-pi-šá-ni-GIRRA lip-šur

You have turned me over to the ghost of ruins, may GIRRA undo this!

a-na sêri ki-di u na-me-e tap-qí-da-in-ni te-pu-šá-ni tu-še-pi-šá-ni-GIRRA lip-šur

You have sent me into open desert to rot, may GIRRA undo this!

a-na dûri ù sa-me-ti tap-qí-da-in-ni te-pu-šá-ni tu-še-pi-šá-ni GIRRA lip-šur

You have pressed me up against the [inner and outer] walls, may GIRRA undo this!

[25] a-na dbe-lit sêri u ba-ma-a-ti tap-qí-da-in-ni te-pu-šá-ni tu-še-pi-šáni-GIRRA lip-šur

You have turned me over to the Mistress of the Mountains, may GIRRA undo this!

a-na utûn la-ab-ti tinûri kinûni KI.UT.BA ù nap-pa-ha-ti tap-qí-da-in-ni-te-pu-šá-ni tu-še-pi-šá-ni GIRRA lip-šur

You have delivered me into a furnace, on the stove-top, into pails of hot embers and coals, may GIRRA undo this!

salmânimeš-ia a-na lúpagri tap-qí-da te-pu-šá-ni tu-še-pi-šá-ni GIRRA lip-šur

You have given [images] of me to the dead, may GIRRA undo this!

salmânimeš-ia a-na lúpagri ta-hi-ra te-pu-šá-ni tu-še-pi-šá-ni GIRRA lip-šur

You have made [images] of me among the dead, may GIRRA undo this!

salmânimeš-ia it-ti lúpagri tuš-ni-il-la te-pu-šá-ni tu-še-pi-šá-ni GIRRA lip-šur

You have placed [images] of me next to the dead, may GIRRA undo this!

[30] salmânimeš-ia ina sûn lúpagri tuš-ni-il-la te-pu-šá-ni tu-še-pi-šá-ni-GIRRA lip-šur

You have placed [images] of me into the hands of the dead, may GIRRA undo this!

salmânimeš-ia ina qimah lúpagri taq-bi-ra te-pu-šá-ni tu-še-pi-šá-ni-GIRRA lip-šur

You have buried [images] of me in the grave of the dead, may GIRRA undo this!

salmânimeš-ia a-na gul-gul-la-ti tap-qí-da te-pu-šá-ni tu-še-pi-šá-ni-GIRRA lip-šur

You have turned [images] of me over to the dead, may GIRRA undo this!

salmânimeš-ia ina igâri tap-ha-a te-pu-šá-ni tu-še-pi-šá-ni GIRRA lipšur

You have locked away [images] of me in the wall-safe, may GIRRA undo this!

salmânimeš-ia ina asquppati tuš-ni-il-la te-pu-šá-ni tu-še-pi-šá-ni-GIRRA lip-šur

You have placed [images] of me at the baneful threshold, may GIRRA undo this!

[35] salmânimeš-ia ina bi-' šá dûri tap-ha-a te-pu-šá-ni tu-še-pi-šá-ni-GIRRA lip-šur

You have locked up [images] of me at the baneful entrance, may GIRRA undo this!

salmânimeš-ia ina ti-tur-ri taq-bi-ra-ma um-ma-nu ú-kab-bí-su te-pu-šáni tu-še-pi- šá-ni GIRRA lip-šur

You have embedded [images] of me on a bridge, causing others to step on me, may GIRRA undo this!

salmânimeš-ia ina bu-ri iqi šá lúašlaki bûra tap-ta-a taq-bi-ra te-pu-šá-ni-tu-še-pi-šá-ni GIRRA lip-šur

You have embedded [images] of me in the wash-house drains, may GIRRA undo this!

salmânimeš-ia ina iqi šá lúlâkuribbi bûra tap-ta-a taq-bi-ra te-pu-šá-ni-tu-še-pi-šá-ni GIRRA lip-šur

You have buried [images] of me in the gardener's [ditch], may GIRRA undo this!

salmânimeš-ia lu-u šá isbîni lu-u šá iserini lu-u šá lipî

...images of me from wood and salt,

lu-u šá ISKUR lu-u šá kuspi
from wax, from seed,
lu-u šá itti lu-u šá titi lu-u šá liši
from asphalt, from clay, from dough;
salmânimeš sir-ri-ia pa-ni-ia u la-ni-ia te-pu-šâ-ma
images, likenesses of my face and form you mold
kalba tu-šá-ki-la šahâ tu-šá-ki-la
then give to a dog and a pig to eat,
issuru tu-šá-ki-la ana nâri taddâa
given to the birds of the sky who drop them in the river;

salmânimeš-ia a-na la-maš-ti mârat da-nim
...images of me to LAMASTU, daughter of ANU,
tap-qí-da te-pu-šá-ni tu-še-pi-šá-ni GIRRA lip-šur
what you have given to do, what others have done for you, may GIRRA undo this!
salmânimeš-ia a-na GIRRA tap-qí-da te-pu-šá-ni tu-še-pi-šá-ni GIRRA lip-šur
...images of me given to GIRRA, you have done this, may GIRRA undo this!
mêmeš-ia it-ti lúpagri tuš-ni-il-la te-pu-šá-ni tu-še-pi-šá-ni GIRRA lipšur
You have poured my [water] in with the dead, may GIRRA undo this!
mêmeš-ia ina sûn lúpagri tuš-ni-il-la te-pu-šá-ni tu-še-pi-šá-ni GIRRA lip-šur
You have poured my [water] in the lap of the dead, may GIRRA undo this!

mêmeš-ia ina qimah l;úpagri taq-bi-ra te-pu-šá-ni tu-še-pi-šá-ni-GIRRA lip-šur
You have poured my [water] into the grave of the dead, may GIRRA undo this!

ina-tim mêmeš-ia taq-bi-ra te-pu-šá-ni tu-še-pi-šá-ni GIRRA lip-šur

You have poured my [water] in the body of the dead, may GIRRA undo this!

ina-tim mêmeš-ia taq-bi-ra te-pu-šá-ni tu-še-pi-šá-ni GIRRA lip-šur

You have poured my [water] in the body of the dead, may GIRRA undo this!

ina-me mêmeš-ia tah-ba-a te-pu-šá-ni tu-še-pi-šá-ni GIRRA lip-šur

You have siphoned the [water] from my body, may GIRRA undo this!

mêmeš-ia ana Gilgameš ta-ad-di-na te-pu-šá-ni tu-še-pi-šá-ni GIRRA lip-šur

To GILGAMESH you have given my water, may GIRRA undo this!

[55] <unreadable text> li-e ta-hi-ra-in-ni te-pu-šá-ni tu-še-pi-šá-ni-GIRRA lip-šur

You have lost my waters to the ditch, may GIRRA undo this!

zikurudâa a-na pa-ni NANNA-SIN te-pu-šá-ni tu-še-pi-šá-ni GIRRA lip-šur

You have slit my throat before NANNA-SIN, may GIRRA undo this!

zikurudâa a-na pa-ni dšul-pa-è-a te-pu-šá-ni tu-še-pi-šá-ni GIRRA lipšur

You have slit my throat before SUL-PA-EA, may GIRRA undo this!

zikurudâa a-na pa-ni MULU-KA-DU-A

You have slit my throat in the starlight of CYGNUS and LACERTA,

zikurudâa <unreadable text> te-pu-šá-ni tu-še-pi-šá-ni GIRRA lip-šur
You have slit my throat... may GIRRA undo this!
GAB TIN taš-<unreadable text in next 6 lines>

[60] meš u uhuli tu-ram-me-ki-in-ni
tap-qi-da
-a-ti tu-še-bi-la
bîtu tu-šá-áš-qi ai
ina pân -zi u bâb bîti ma-
In front of the entrance gate of the house,

[65] ina pân ib-ri tap-pi u ki-na-at-ti KI.MINA
In front of friends, companions and servants [of the house],
ina pân abi u ummi ahi u ahati mâri u mârti KI.MINA
In front of parents and siblings [of the house],
ina pân bîti u bâbi ardi u amti sih-ri u ra-bi šá bîti KI.MINA
In front of the house and gate, servants, both small and large [of the house],
elî a-me-ri-ia tu-šam-ri-si-in-ni....
You made me ugly to all those who behold me.
ak-ta-mi-ku-nu-ši ak-ta-si-ku-nu-ši at-ta-din-ku-nu-ši
I have bound you, tied you up and delivered you over

[70] ana GIRRA qa-mi-i qa-li-i ka-si-i
to GIRRA, who burns, incinerates, binds up
ka-ši-du šá kaššapâtimeš
and seizes the sorceress.
GIRRA qa-mu-ú li-pat-tir rik-si-ku-nu
GIRRA, burn away your knots, undo your
li-pa-áš-šir kiš-pi-ku-nu li-na-as si-ir-qi-ku-nu
enchantments and untie your ropes,

ina qí-bit MARDUK mâr dé-a apqalli
by the decree of MARDUK, son of ENKI the Wise Father of Magicians,

u GIRRA a-ri-ru ap-qal mâr da-nim qar-du SU.EN
and GIRRA, praised and wise – born of ANU!

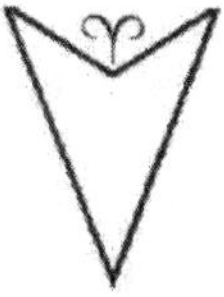

ÉN at-ti man-nu kassaptušá zitarrutâa êpušaša
Who are you, sorcer[ess]? Who has committed the murder?
lu-u ib-ru lu-u tap-pu-u
Whether companion or neighbor,
lu-u ahu lu-u it-ba-ru
whether family or friend,
lu-u ú-ba-ra lu-u mâr âli
whether foreigner or native,

lu-u mu-du-u lu-u la mûdû
whether known or unknown
lu-u lúkaššapu lu-u kaššaptu
whether sorcerer or sorceress,
lu-u zikaru lu-u sinništu lu-ú hab-lu lu-ú ha-bil-ti
whether man or woman, murderer or murderess,
lu-u lúkur-gar-ru-u lu-u sah-hi-ru
whether *kugarru*-priest or *sahhiru*-priestess,
lu-u ... lu-u nar-šin-du-u lu-u muš-lahhêe
whether... or a *narsindu* or snake-charmer,

[85] lu-u a-gu-gi-lu-u lišanu nukur-tum šá ina mâti ibašši
whether an *agugilu* or an foreign traveller...

<signficant unreadable text in next 19 lines>

-tu giškak-ku-šu li-še-bir-ma
-mid-su-nu-te SU.EN

ÉN nir-ti-ià kaššapti-ia u ku-šá-pa-ti-ia
is

[90] maa-
-si-šú-nu-ti
a-ta-am-ma-ak-šú-nu-ti kia-
šak-kan-šú-nu-ti ana pi-i GIRRA qa-mi-i
qa-li-i ka-si-i ka-ši-du

[95] šá kaššapatimeš SU.EN
ÉN šá dšamšiši man-nu abu-šú man-nu ummu-šu
man-nu a-hat-su-ma šu-ú da-a-a-nu
šá MARDUK u NANNA-SIN ilu
git-ma-lu

[100] SAMAS
ù ši-i diš-tar a-hat-su-ma šu-u da-a-a-nu
kiš-pi ú-hal-laq
ep-šu bar-tum âmat lemut-tim
ú-pa-šar - - SU.EN

ÉN i-pu-šá-ni i-te-ni-ip-pu-šá-ni
It hexes. It vexes, unceasingly.
gu-ti-e-ti e-la-ma-a-ti
The CUTHITES, the ELAMITES,
ma-rat ha-ni-gal-bat-a-ti
the daughters of the *hanigalbatians*,
6 ina mâti i-rak-ka-sa-a-ni rik-si
the six on dry earth bind knots,
6 riksi-ši-na 7 pit-ru-ú-a
six are their knots, seven is my untying.

šá mûša ip-pu-sa-nim-ma
What they tie in the night,
šá kal u-mu a-pa-áš-šar-ši-na-ti
I untie in the day.
šá kal u-mu ip-pu-šá-nim-ma
What they tie in daylight,
šá mûša a-pa-áš-šar-ši-na-ti
I untie in the nighttime.
a-šak-kan-ši-na-a-ti ana pi-i GIRRA qa-mi-i
I turn them over to the burning, GIRRA,

qa-li-i ka-si-i ka-ši-du
incinerating, binding and seizing
šá kaššapatimeš SU.EN
the sorcer[esses]!

ÉN ru-'ú-a kaš-šá-pat ana-ku pa-ši-ra-ak
My anathema is a witch! I am released!
kassaptukas-šá-pat ana-ku pa-ši-ra-ak
The witch is a wicked witch, I am released!
kassaptue-la-ma-a-ti ana-ku pa-ši-ra-ak
The witch is an ELAMITE, I am released!

kassaptuqu-ta-a-ti ana-ku pa-ši-ra-ak
The witch is a CUTHITE, I am released!
kassaptusu-ta-a-ti ana-ku pa-ši-ra-ak
The witch is of the SUTI-tribes, I am released!
kassaptulul-lu-ba-a-ti ana-ku pa-ši-ra-ak
The witch is a *lulluban*, I am released!
kassaptuha-bi-gal-ba-at ana-ku pa-ši-ra-ak
The witch is a *hanigalbatan*, I am released!
kassaptua-gu-gi-lat ana-ku pa-ši-ra-ak
The witch is an *agugiltu*, I am released!

kassaptunar-šin-da-at ana-ku pa-ši-ra-ak
The witch is an *narsindatu*, I am released!
kassaptumušlahhat ana-ku pa-ši-ra-ak
The witch is a snake-charmer, I am released!
kassaptueš-še-ba-a-ti ana-ku pa-ši-ra-ak
The witch is a priestess of magick, I am released!
kassaptuqur-qur-ra-a-ti ana-ku pa-ši-ra-ak
The witch is a metallurgist, I am released!
kassaptuši-i râbis bâbi-ia ana-ku pa-ši-ra-ak
The witch is a spoke on my gate, I am released!

kassaptumârat âli-ia ana-ku pa-ši-ra-ak
The witch is a neighbor of mine, I am released!
áš-pur a-na e-rib dšamši salmânimeš-si-na il-qu-tu-ú-ni
I have gathered her [images] and sent them to the west.

šá u kaššapâtimeš salmânimeš-ši-na
The figures of the seven and the seven witches
ana GIRRA ap-qid
to GIRRA, I deliver.
ana ú-tu-ni a-lik-ti a-šar-rap-ši-na-ti
In a portable kiln I have burned them.

[135] GIBIL qu-mi lúkaššapi u kaššapti
GIBIL, burn the evil warlock and wicked witch!
GIBIL qu-li lúkaššapi u kaššapti
GIBIL, incinerate my warlock and witch!
GIBIL qu-mi-ši-na-a-ti
GIBIL, burn them completely!
GIBIL qu-li-ši-na-a-ti
GIBIL, incinerate them completely!
GIBIL kušus-si-na-a-ti
GIBIL, seize the whole of their being!

[140] GIBIL a-ru-uh-ši-na-a-ti
GIBIL, devour them completely!
GIBIL šu-ta-bil-si-na-a-ti
GIBIL, remove them away from here!
ez-zu GIBIL li-ni-ih-ka-na-ši
Roaring GIBIL, please calm down!
GIBIL lu-li-mu... li-ki-na-ši
GIBIL, [save me and] calm yourself!
lúkaššapu u kassaptue-piš u e-piš-tum
The sorcerer and sorceress, the enchanter and enchantress,

[145] šu-nu lu-u ... -kam-ma
may they truly [burn out completely]!
ana-ku mêmeš mîli-ma
though I let loose the floodwater

lu-u-ba-'-ši-na-a-ti SU.ÉN
to shower down upon them!

ÉN e-piš-tum ù muš-te-piš-tum
(First line of the next tablet in the series.)

tuppu kam ma-aq-lu-ú
(Here ends the fourth tablet of the MAQLU.)

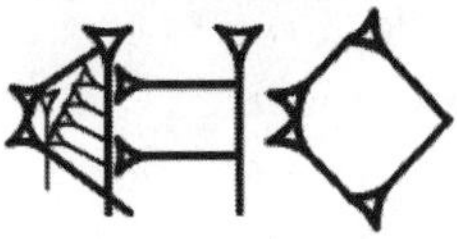

Tablet V

ÉN e-piš-ti ù muš-te-piš-ti
My enchanter and my enchantress
áš-bat ina silli a-ma-ri ša libitti
sit in the shade of a stoop made of clay bricks.
áš-bat-ma ip-ši-ia ip-pu-šá i-ban-na-a salmânimeš-ia
[She] sits doing tricks, fashioning [images] of me.
a-šap-pa-rak-kim-ma šamhašutu u SAMAS-šammu
I send you thyme and sesame [literally '*sunflower*'].

[5] ú-sap-pa-ah kiš-pi-ki ú-tar amâtimeš-ki ana pî-ki
Your sorcery is anathema to me, your words fall back into your mouth!
ip-ši te-pu-ši lu-u šá at-tu-ki
The tricks you 'turn' now turn against you!
salmânimeš tab-ni-i lu-u šá tè-me-ki
The [images] you made of me, may they now resemble you!

mêmeš tah-bi-i lu-u šá ra-ma-ni-ki
The waters [of mine] you siphoned are your own!
ši-pat-ki ai iq-ri-ba amâtmeš-ki ai ik-šu-da-in-ni
Your magick spell does not come close to me, your Word cannot reach where I [stand]!

[10] ina qí-bit dé-a SAMAS u MARDUK u rubâti dbe-lit ilê SU.EN
By the incantation of ENKI, SAMAS and MARDUK [and among them] the Lady of the Gods [BELIT]!

ÉN man-nu pû ip-til utteta ú-qas-sir
Who has tried to [commit the unthinkable]?
ana šamêe kiš-pi ana irsitimtim bar-ta êpušuš
Who has ever bewitched Heaven or performed magick against the Earth?
ana šamirri ilimeš rabûtimeš ip-šá bar-ta
Against the IRRI [*erra, NERGAL*], the Great Gods, who has ever cast magick [upon these],
amât limuttimtim man-nu ú-qar-rib
or spoken evil words against them?

[15] ki-ma pû la ip-pat-til uttatu la uk-ta-as-sa-ru
Just as the unthinkable cannot be done, neither can
ana šamêe kiš-pi ana irsitimtim bar-tu la in-ni-ip-pu-šú
magick be done against Heaven or Earth.
ana mârat ilimeš rabûtimeš
[And so as] the daughter of the Great Gods;
ip-šá bar-tum amat limuttimtim lâ itehu lâ i-qar-ru-bu
magick, sorcery, baneful spells do not come close;
ip-šá bar-tum amât limuttimtim lâ iteha
[so too should] magick, sorcery, baneful spells not

[20] lâ i-qar-ru-ba ia-a-ši SU.EN
come close to me!

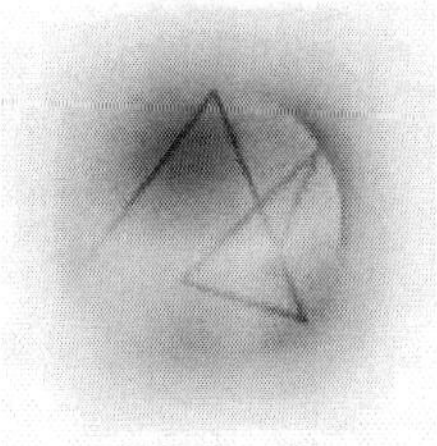

ÉN du-un-na-nu du-un-na-nu pârisis pu-ru-us-si-e-ni
DUNNANU, DUNANNU, you who is fated our decisions,
i-na ma-har NUSKU u GIRRA šu-bil-te šak-na-at
In front of NUSKU and GIRRA my [image] is placed.
al-ki na-bal-kàt-tum šu-um-ri na-bal-kàt-tum
Come forth and attack! Rage on! Avenge me! Attack!
i-na na-sa-ah šêpê šá lúkaššapi-ia
When you tear off the feet of my sorcerer

u kaššapti-ia šêpê-ki šuk-ni
and my sorceress, stamp your own feet down.
lillu li-bi-il-ma kassaptuana da-ai-ni-šá
May the sorcer[ess] be dragged before the Judge!
daianu-šá kîma nêši li-sa-a elî-šá
May [her] judge roar like a lion [at her]!
lim-has lêt-sa li-tir amât-sa ana pî-šá
May he strike her face and cause her words to turn back into her mouth!
e-piš-ti ù muš-te-piš-ti
Of the sorceress and 'greater' sorceress,

ki-ma šamnini li-nu-šú kiš-pu-šá
Like mint, may her magick sting her!
ki-ma šamazupiri li-sap-pi-ru-ši kiš-pu-šá
Like saffron, may her magick scratch at her!
ki-ma šamsahli li-is-hu-lu-ši kiš-pu-šá
Like mustard, may her magick penetrate her!
ki-ma šam-KUR.ZI.SAR li-sa-am-mu-si kiš-pu-šá
Like the weed [*kurzisar*] , may her magick bind her up!
ki-ma šamkasi li-ik-su-ši kiš-pu-šá
Like cassia, may her magick tie [them] up!

ki-ma šamhašûti li-haš-šu-ši kiš-pu-šá
Like thyme, may her magick bind them up!
ki-ma kit-mi li-ik-tu-mu-ši kiš-pu-šá
Like alum, may her magick cover them up!
ki-ma šamirri li-ru-ru-ši kiš-pu-šá
Like pumpkin-vine, may her magick strangle them up!
ki-ma šamnuhurti lit-tah-hi-ra šapâtimeš-šá
Like *asafoetida*, may [their] lips swell up!

e-piš-ti ù muš-te-piš-ti
Of the sorceress and the 'greater' sorceress,

lib-bal-kit-si sûqu ù su-lu-ú
may the street and pathway give out around them!
lib-bal-kit-si ib-ra-tum ù ni-me-di-šá
May the room and chair give out beneath them!
lib-bal-ki-tu-ši-ma ilimeš šá sêri u âli
May the God of the desert and city fall upon them!
kassaptukima kalbi ina hatti kima an-du-hal-lat ina kir-ban-ni
May someone chase the sorceress about like a dog with a stick or like a serpent on the earth.
ki-ma kib-si immeri li-sa-am-me-ku-ši-ma li-ti-qu-ši
[like a] chase through a sheep-path, pass over them!

ki-ma qur-sin-ni imêri ina sûqi e-te-qu lik-kil-me-ši
[like a] donkey's feet when crossing the street, may someone look upon them.
e-piš-ti ù muš-te-piš-ti
Of the sorceress and 'greater' sorceress,
ina bi-rit kalbêmeš li-su-ru ku-lu-lu-šá
may their crowns fall among dogs,
ina bi-rit ku-lu-lu-šá li-su-ru kalbêmeš
may dogs dance about with their headbands!
e-li-šá qul-mu-ú li-su-ru
And may the axe dance down upon them!

ki-ma piqan sabiti qu-tur-šá li-ib-li SU.EN
[like a] gazelle having a bowel-movement, may their breath be taken away!

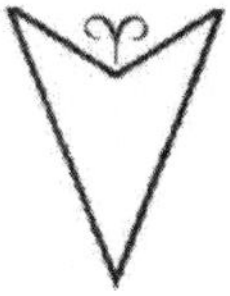

ÉN at-ti man-nu kassaptušá tetenîpu-šášá 3 arhêmeš 10 u-me mišil u-me

What is your name sorcer[ess], who has worked your spell unceasingly for 3 months plus 10 and a half days?

ana-ku a-na-áš-šá-kim-ma riqqukukru ta-nat šadî

I raise up the pride of the mountains,

šamhašûtu ti-'-ut ma-a-ti

thyme and the prepared foods of the earth,

pitiltu pitiltu šá qašdatimeš terinnatu terinnatu šá še-am ma-la-ti

acorns and pinecones, that which is full of seed.

[55] an-nu-ú šá lúkaššapi-ia u kaššapti-ia hi-pa-a ri-kiš-šu-un

Yes, my sorcerer and sorceress; I know thee; Come, break their knots,

tir-ra kiš-pu-šá ana me-hi-e amâtimeš-šá ana šá-a-ri

turn their spells into storm, their words to wind!

li-in-na-áš-pu kiš-pu-šá kîma pû liq-qal-pu kîma šûmi

May their deceit be blown away as dust, peeled away like layers of garlic [onion],

liš-šá-ah-tu kima suluppi lip-pa-áš-ru kima pitilti

beaten to a pulp like date-fruit and scattered like acorns [seeds]!

ina qí-bit ISTAR ddumu-zi dna-na-a be-lit ra-a-mi

By the decree of ISHTAR, TAMMUZ, NANAYA, the Mistress of Divine Love,

[60] ù dka-ni-sur-ra be-lit kaššapâtimeš TU.EN
and of *kanisurra*, the Mistress of Sorceresses!

ÉN zêru šá te-pu-šá-ni tu-še-pi-šá-ni ana muh-hi-ku-nu
The hate conjured in your magick, you conjure it against yourself.

zitarrutâa šá te-pu-šá-ni tu-še-pi-šá-ni ana muh-hi-ku-nu , dipalâa-šá te-pu-šá-ni tu-še-pi-šá-ni ana muh-hi-ku-nu kadibbidâa šá te-pu-šá-ni tu-še-pi-šá-ni-ana muh-hi-ku-nu
The murder you have conjured, you have conjured against yourself; the chaos you have conjured, you have conjured against yourself; the disease you have conjured, you have conjured against yourself;

KUS.HUNGA šá te-pu-šá-ni tu-še-pi-šá-ni ana muh-hi-ku-nu dububbâ šá te-pu-šá- ni tu-še-pi-šá-ni ana muh-hi-ku-nu
The *kushunga* you have conjured, you have conjured against yourself; the calamity you have conjured, you have conjured against yourself!

utukku limnu tu-šá-as-bi-ta-in-ni utukku limnu li-is-bat-ku-nu-ši
The evil *utukku* daemon that you allowed to seize me; may the evil *utukku* seize you!

[65] alû limnu tu-šá-as-bi-ta-in-ni alû limnu li-is-bat-ku-nu-ši

The evil *alu* daemon that you allowed to seize me; may the evil *alu* seize you!

etimmu limnu tu-šá-as-bi-ta-in-ni etimmu limnu li-is-bat-ku-nu-ši

The evil spirit that you allowed to seize me; may the evil spirit seize you!

gallû limnu tu-šá-as-bi-ta-in-ni gallû limnu li-is-bat-ku-nu-ši

The evil *gallu* spirit that you allowed to seize me; may the evil *gallu* spirit seize you!

ilu limnu tu-šá-as-bi-ta-in-ni ilu limnu li-is-bat-ku-nu-ši

The evil god that you allowed to seize me; may the evil god seize you!

râbisu limnu tu-šá-as-bi-ta-in-ni râbisu limnu li-is-bat-ku-nu-ši

The evil *rabisu* watcher that you allowed to seize me; may the evil *rabisu* seize you!

[70] lamaštu labasu ahhazu tu-šá-as-bi-ta-in-ni lamaštu labasu ahhazu-li-is-bat-ku-nu-ši

***Lamastu, Labasu,* those you allowed to seize me, may *Lamastu* and *Labasu* seize you!**

lúlilû flilitu ardat lili tu-šá-as-bi-ta-in-ni lúlilû flilitu ardat lili li-is- -bat-ku-nu-ši

***Lilu, Lilitu,* those nightmares you allowed to seize me, may *Lilu, Lilitu* and those nightmares seize you!**

ina ni-ši u ma-mit tu-qat-ta-in-ni ina ni-ši u ma-mit pa-gar-ku-nu liq-ti

You seek to destroy me by covenants and magick words, may your life end by covenants and magick words.

uz-zi ili šarri BELI u rubî ia-a-ši taš-ku-na-ni
The wrath of God, King and judges you have suffered me,
uz-zi ili šarri BELI u rubî a-na ka-a-šu-nu liš-šak-nak-ku-nu-ši
may the wrath of God, King and judges cause you suffering!

a-šu-uš-tu a-ru-ur-tu hu-us qis lìb-bi gi-lit-tú
Pain. Famine. Breaking of the body. Uncontrolled trembling;
pi-rit-ti a-dir-ti ia-a-ši taš-ku-na-ni
Fear and depression – all these you have planned for me;
a-šu-uš-tu a-ru-ur-tu hu-us qis lìb-bi gi-lit-tú
May pain, famine, body-breaking, uncontrolled trembling,
pi-rit-ti a-dir-tu ana ka-a-šú-nu liš-šak-nak-ku-nu-ši
fear and depression – and all such be planned for you!
aq-mu-ku-nu-ši ina kibrit ellititi u tâbat amurri
I have burned you with pure sulfur and salt [from the west];
al-qut qu-tur-ku-nu ik-kib šamêe
I have siphoned away your breath to paint the sky;
ip-še-te-ku-nu i-tu-ra-ni-ku-nu-ši SU.EN
Your plans for me have turned against you!

ÉN at-ti man-nu kassaptušá kîma šûti ik-ki-mu ûmi 15 kam
Whoever you are, my sorcer[ess], you who blow like the south-wind on the 15th day,
ti-il-ti u-me im-ba-ru šá-na-at na-al-ši
You, whose storm-cloud has gathered for 9 days, whose rain-showers have fallen for a year,
urpata iq-su-ra-am-ma iz-zi-za ia-a-ši
You, who has conjured clouds to stand over me:

[85] a-te-ba-ak-kim-ma ki-ma gal-la-ab šamêe šâriltânu
I rise up to fight you, like the Shredder of the Heavens, the north-wind!
ú-sap-pa-ah ur-pa-ta-ki ú-hal-laq ûm-ki
I scatter your clouds to the wind and destroy your storms!
ú-sap-pa-ah kiš-pi-ki ša tak-ki-mi mu-ša u ur-ra
I scatter the witchcraft you brought unceasingly against me both night and day,
ù na-áš-pa-rat zitarruti šá tal-tap-pa-ri ia-a-ši
and the accessories [emissaries] of your evil that you unceasingly sent to fight me!

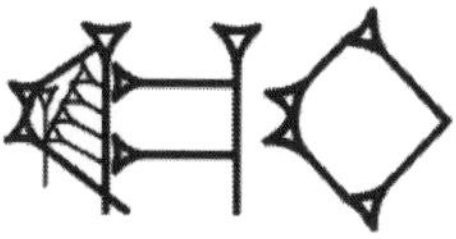

*ÉN šá-ru-uh la-a-ni šá-ru-uh la-a-ni**

* Translation Note: As the MAQLU series progresses they become increasingly 'broken', 'damaged' or 'fragmentary' in even the best tablet-renditions available. As such, these parts will not be translated for this text if found too sparse.

al-lal-lu <unreadable text in next 26 lines>
na-mu-ú -
e-piš -
kaš-šá-pu -
a-na d-

ÉN šir'anêmeš tu-kas-si-rasalmânimeš
tug-gi-ra tu-kas-sa-aki-
sir tak-su-ra-ni ki-
GIRRA a-ri-ru li-NUSKU
ANU-

e-piš te-pu-šá-ni ana muh-hi-ku-nupa-
áš-ru kiš-pu-ú-aina
mêmeš ta-bu-tiana-
ku e-te-lil e-te-bi-ib ÉN
at-tu-nu mêmeš-

ta-at-ta-nab-lak-ka-tatu-
hap-pa-a ka-ramêmeš
-umêmeš
tâmtiih-
bu-nik-ku-nu-ši

apkallu šu-ut eri-duina
te-šú-nu elli te- tuk-sakima
ina te-šú-nulib-
bi lúkaššapi-ia u kaššapti-iaana-
ku ina qí-bit d-

a-sal-lah lib-ba-ku-nua-
sal-lah la-'-me-ku-nuina
qí-bit dé-a SAMAS u MARDUK u rubâti dbe-lit ilê SU.EN

ÉN e-piš-ú-a e-piš-tu-u-a
Evil warlock. Wicked witch.
kaš-šá-pu-u-a kaš-šap-tu-u-a
Evil sorcerer and sorceress.

[120] šá ik-pu-du libbu-ku-nu limuttimtim
You, whose heart has conjured evil,
taš-te-ni-'-a ru-hi-e sab-ru-ti
who have sought out the evil magick,
ina up-šá-še-e la tâbutimeš tu-sab-bi-ta bir-ki-ia
who has bound my lefs with evil incantations.
ana-ku ana pu-uš-šur kiš-pi-ia u ru-hi-e-a
To break my spell and turn your enchantment, I have turned
ina a-mat dea u dasari-lú-du GIRRA as-sah-ri
toward the [word] of ENKI and MARDUK [*asariludu*] and GIRRA.

[125] ina mêmeš ša naqbi lìb-ba-ku-nu ú-ni-ih
In water-springs I have brought peace to your heart;
ka-bat-ta-ku-nu ú-bal-li
I have soothed your upset liver;
si-ri-ih lib-bi-ku-nu ú-še-si
I have dispelled your quick-anger;

te-en-ku-nu ú-šá-an-ni
I have confounded your mind;
mi-lik-ku-nu as-pu-uh
I have destroyed your plans;

[130] kiš-pi-ku-nu aq-lu
I have burned your spells;
kip-di lib-bi-ku-nu ú-mat-ti-ku-nu-ši
I have numbered the days of your life.
idiqlat u puratta la te-bi-ra-ni
[The] Tigris and Euphrates [rivers], you will not pass!
iqa u palga la te-it-ti-qa-ni
[The] moat and aqueduct, you will not pass!
dûra u sa-me-ti la tab-ba-lak-ki-ta-ni
[The inner and outer] walls, you will not climb!

[135] abulla u ne-ri-bi-e la tir-ru-ba-ni
[The] gate or entry to the place, you will not pass!
kiš-pi-ku-nu ai ithunimeš-ni
Your spells will not approach me!
a-ma-at-ku-nu ai ik-šu-da-in-ni
Your word cannot reach where I stand!
ina qí-bit dé-a SAMAS u MARDUK rubâti dbe-lit ilê SU.EN
By the decree of ENKI, SAMAS, MARDUK and the Supreme Mistress of the Gods!

ÉN iz-zi-tu-nu šam-ra-tu-nu qas-sa-tu-nu
Fierce, raging, ferocious,

gap-šá-tu-nu nad-ra-tu-nu lim-ni-tu-nu
Overbearing, violent, evil are you!
šá la dé-a man-nu ú-na-ah-ku-nu-ši
Who but ENKI can calm you?
šá la dasari-lú-du man-nu ú-šap-sah-ku-nu-ši
Who but MARDUK [*asalluhi*] can cool you down?
dé-a li-ni-ih-ku-nu-ši
ENKI, may he calm you!
dasari-lú-du li-šap-ših-ku-nu-ši
MARDUK [*asalluhi*], may he cool you down!

mêmeš pî-ia mêmeš pi-ku-nu i-šâ-tu
Water is my mouth; fire is your mouth:
pî-ia pî-ku-nu li-bal-li
[May] my mouth extinguish your mouth!
tu-u šá pî-ia tu-u šá pî-ku-nu li-bal-li
[May] the curse of my mouth extinguish the curse of your mouth!
kip-di šá lìb-bi-ia li-bal-la-a kip-di šá lìb-bi-ku-nu
[May] my desired plans extinguish your desired plans!

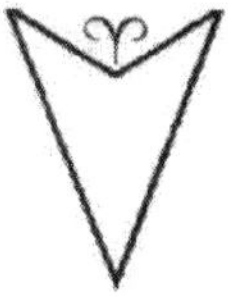

ÉN ak-bu-us gallâ-ai-
[*affirmation*] I have taken my enemy down in front of GIRRA!

[150] at-bu-uh gi-ra-ai ahi-
I have killed my enemy by the sacred word!
na mah-ri qu-ra-di GIRRA-
All of this in front of the mighty GIRRA [I have done]!

ÉN hu-la zu-ba u i-ta-at-tu-ka
Scatter, flow and drift away from here!
qu-tur-ku-nu li-tel-li šamêe
May your words float away to the sky!
la-'-me-ku-nu li-bal-li dšamšiši
May the sun extinguish the radiance of your ashes!

[155] lip-ru-us ha-ai-ta-ku-nu mâr dé-a mašmašu TU.EN
May your spy be slain, by [MARDUK] the son of ENKI, the Magician!

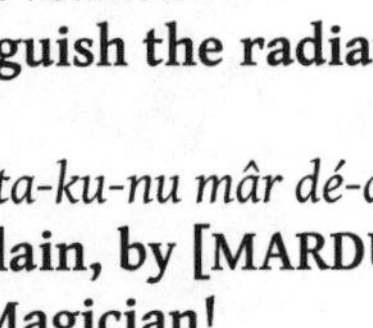

ÉN šadûu lik-tùm-ku-nu-ši
May the mountain cover you!
šadûu lik-la-ku-nu-ši
May the mountain hold you back!
šadûu li-ni-ih-ku-nu-ši
May the mountain calm you down!
šadûu li-ih-si-ku-nu-ši
May the mountain overpower you!

šadûu li-te-'-ku-nu-ši
May the mountain swallow you up!
šadûu li-ni-'-ku-nu-ši
May the mountain pass reject you!
šadûu li-nir-ku-nu-ši
May the mountain cliff kill you!
šadûu li-qat-tin-ku-nu-ši
May the mountain wastelands make you thin!
šadûu dan-nu elî-ku-nu lim-qut
May the [mighty] mountain avalanche fall upon you!

ina zumri-ia lu-u tap-par-ra-sa-ma SU.EN
Indeed, you shall be shaken from my body!

ÉN i-sa-a i-sa-a ri-e-qa ri-e-qa
Go away! Go away! Be gone! Be gone!
bi-e-šá bi-e-šá hi-il-qa hi-il-qa
Stay away! Stay away! Flee! Flee!
dup-pi-ra at-la-ka i-sa-a u ri-e-qa
Get off! Go away! Stay away! Be gone!
limuttu-ku-nu ki-ma qut-ri li-tel-li šamêe
Your evil spell, like smoke, may it rise ever skyward into nothing!

ina zumri-ia i-sa-a
From my body, keep off!
ina zumri-ia ri-e-qa
From my body, be gone!
ina zumri-ia bi-e-šá
From my body, depart!
ina zumri-ia hi-il-qa
From my body, flee!
ina zumri-ia dup-pi-ra
From my body, get off!

ina zumri-ia at-la-ka
From my body, go away!
ina zumri-ia la tatârâ
From my body, turn away!
na zumri-ia la tetehêe
My body, do not approach!
ina zumri-ia la taqarubâ
My body, do not come near!
ina zumri-ia la tasaniqâqa
My body, do not touch!

ni-iš SAMAS kabti lu ta-ma-tu-nu
By the breath of SAMAS, Radiant One, you are commanded!
ni-iš dé-a BEL naqbi lu ta-ma-tu-nu
By the breath of ENKI, Lord of the Deep, you are commanded!
ni-iš dasari-lú-du maš-maš ilimeš lu ta-ma-tu-nu
By the breath of MARDUK [*asalluhi*], Magician of the Gods, you are commanded!
ni-iš GIRRA qa-mi-ku-nu lu ta-ma-tu-nu
By the breath of GIRRA, your Executioner, you are commanded!
ina zumri-ia lu-u tap-par-ra-sa-ma SU.EN
Indeed you shall be kept from my body!

ÉN ENLIL qaqqadi-ia pa-nu-u-a u-mu
(*The first line of the next tablet in the series.*)

tuppu Vkam ma-aq-lu-ú
(*Here ends the fifth tablet of the MAQLU.*)

Tablet VI

ÉN den-lil qaqqadi-ia pa-nu-ú-a u-mu
ENLIL is my head, the face that meets the day,
duraš ilu git-ma-lu la-mas-sat pa-ni-ia
URAS, the 'perfect god' is my protecting face,
kišadi-ia ul-lu šá dnin-lil
My neck – the necklace of NINLIL,
idâmeš-ai dgam-lum šá NANNA-SIN amurri
My arms – the crescent swords of NANNA-SIN,

ubânâtumeš-ú-a isbînu esemtu IGIGI
My fingers become *tamarisk* [of ANU], my bones become the IGIGI;
la ú-šá-as-na-qa ru-hi-e a-na zu-um-ri-ia
They do not allow sorcery to penetrate my body.
LUGAL-edin-na dla-ta-raq irti-ia
***Lugaledinna* and *Latark* are my chest,**
kin-sa-ai dmu-úh-ra šêpâII-ai šá ittanallakaka
My knees – *Muhra*, my feet which carry me –
ka-li-ši-na lu lah-mu
are each *Lahmu*.

at-ta man-nu ilu lim-nu šá lúkaššapi u kaššapti
What is your name, Evil God, you whom my sorcerer and sorceress
iš-pu-ru-niš-šú a-na dâki-ia
have conjured to kill me?
lu-ú e-ri-ta la tal-la-ka
When you arise, do not move!
lu-ú sal-la-ta la te-tib-ba-a
When you are asleep, do not awaken!
amâtemeš-ka lu ishašhuru ina pân ili u šarri li-nu-šú
[May] your words become a bitter apple for God and King!

ul-te-sib ina bâbi-ia LUGAL-gir-ra ilu dan-nu
I set at my door, Mighty GIRRA [*lugal-girra*], avenger of gods'
sukkal ilimeš dpap-sukkal
and the messenger of gods, NABU [*papsukkal*] also.
li-du-ku lúkaššapi u kaššapti
They may kill my sorcerer and sorceress;
li-tir-ru amât-sa a-na pî-šá SU.EN
They may turn their words back in their mouth!

ÉN <fragmentary intro> e-piš-ta qu-um-qu-um-ma-tum

kassaptukud-dim-ma-tum
e-piš-ti eš-še-bu-tum
ummu e-piš-ti-ia nar-šin-da-tum
am-me-ni tu-ub-ba-li napištiti ana ma-al-ki
ana-ku a-na pu-sur kiš-pi-ki šam- na-šá-ku

riqqukukru šá šadî -meš ka- ... [TU.EN]

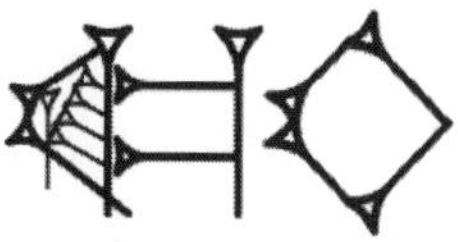

ÉN riqqukukru-ma riqqukukru
Chicory, chicory!*
riqqukukru ina šadânimeš ellûtimeš qud-du-šu-ti
Chicory from the brilliant divine mountains!
sihrûtimeš tir-hi šá e-ni-ti
Small *tirhu*-vessel of the priestess,
sihrâtimeš terinnâtimeš šá qa-aš-da-a-ti
Small pinecones of *hierodule* [*qasdati*],

al-ka-nim-ma šá lúkaššapi-ia u kaššapti-ia
come: of my sorcerer and sorceress
dan-nu hipameš rikis-sa
break their charged knots!

---

* Editor's Note: The *chicory* is a usually a bright blue hue rarely found in nature – though it may also be white or pinkish. It has both dietary and medicinal properties for indigenous cultures (usually from its root) and became popular (prized) as a coffee-additive once the popularity of 'bean-drinks' rose during the "Middle Ages."

tir-ra kiš-pi-ša a-na me-hi-e amâtemeš-šá ana šâri
Turn their magick wild on them, [turn their] words into wind!
li-in-ni-eš-pu kiš-pi-ša ki-ma pû
May their sorcery be blown away on them like granules!
li-ša-as-li-mu-ši ki-ma di-iq-me-en-ni
May [their sorceries] make them black like ash!

[35] ki-ma libitti igâri liš-hu-hu kiš-pu-šá
May their spells break apart over the wall!
šá kaššapti-ia lip-pa-tir rikis lib-bi-šá
May the heart of my sorceress be melted away!

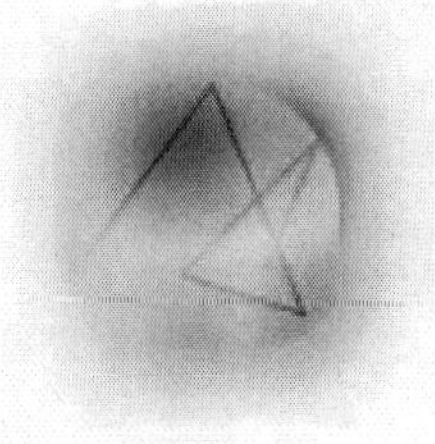

ÉN riqqukukru-ma riqqukukru
Chicory, chicory!
riqqukukru ina šadânimeš ellûtimeš qud-du-šu-ti
Chicory from the brilliant divine mountains!
sihrûtimeš tir-hi šá e-ni-ti
Small *tirhu*-vessel of the priestess,

[40] sihrâtimeš terinnâtimeš šá qa-aš-da-a-ti
Small pinecones of *hierodule* [*qasdati*],
al-ka-nim-ma šá lúkaššapi-ia u kaššapti-ia
come: of my sorcerer and sorceress

dan-nu hipâa rikis-sa
break their charged knots;
ù mimma ma-la te-pu-šá nu-tir a-na šâri
and everything you have bewitched, we turn into wind!

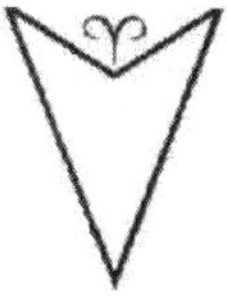

ÉN e kaššapti-ia e-li-ni-ti-ia
My sorceress, my nightmare!

[45] -a-bu la taš-ku-ni tu-qu-un-tu
You have not given up your confounding!
am-me-ni ina bîti-ki i-qat-tur qut-ru
Why does smoke still rise from your house?
a-šap-pa-rak-kim-ma -ti
I am sending you my evil spell!
ú-sap-pah kiš-pi-ki ú-tar amâtemeš-ki ana pî-ki
I destroy your deceit! I destroy your mouth!

ÉN la-am dnin-gir-su ina šadî il-su-u da-la-la
In front of NINGIRSU, in the mountains, a divine song of victory was raised,

la-am kal i-lu-u ana na-kas isbîni
in front of everyone, it raised up and cut *tamarisk*.
kassaptušá ana annanna apil annanna tu-kap-pa-ti abnêmeš
Damn the sorceress who gathers stone [images] against __ son of __,
taš-te-ni-'-e li-mut-ta
and prepare evil sorcery,
a-za-qa-kim-ma kima iltani amurri
I blow on you like the cold north-wind and piercing west-wind!
ú-sap-pah urpata-ki ú-hal-laq u-um-ki
I destroy the clouds of your enchantment and clear away your bad weather,

ù mimma ma-la te-pu-ši ú-tar a-na šâri
and I turn everything you have bewitched into wind!

ÉN e kassaptuú-kaš-šip-an-ni
<unreadable text in next lines> -tum ú-ri-ih-ha-an-ni
- -tum iš-bu-šu epirhi.a šêpêII-ia
- -tum il-qu-ú sillu ina igâri

SAMAS u BEL ummânâtihi.a dé-a BEL šîmâtimeš
dasari-lú-du BEL a-ši-pu-ti
mah-sa lêt-sa tir-ra amât-sa ana pî-šá
e-piš-tum ù muš-te-piš-tum
- lipû šipâtimeš lubarêmeš batqûti

kima qaqqad riqqukukri
a-na a-ha-meš la i-qar-ri-bu
kiš-pu-šá ru-hu-šá ru-su-šá up-šá-šu-šá lem-nu-ti
lâ itehhûmeš-ni lâ i-qar-ri-bu-ni ia-a-ši SU.EN

ÉN at-ta e šá te-pu-ši ka-la-a-ma
You who conjures all types of magick,

min-mu-u te-pu-ši ia-a-ši u šim-ti-ia
what you have bewitched, me and my [image],
riqqukukru šá šadîi ihtepi rikis-ki
chicory from the mountain will break your knots!
šá imitti-ki u šumêli-ki šâru lit-bal TU.EN
May the wind blow away what is left [and right] of you!

ÉN kibri-dit ellitu mârat šamêe rabûtimeš ana-ku
I am pure sufur, I am born of the Daughter of the Heavens,
da-nim ib-na-ni-ma dé-a den-lil ú-še-ri-du-ni-
ANU created me, ENKI and ENLIL brought me down to this planet...

e-piš-tu-a ki-a-am tepuši-in-ni......

<unreadable text in next 8 lines> -ri-du mu šamêe- ma-la
šêpê-ia ki-bi-
- bi-ta - na-dâtat šipat-su šá apqal ili SU.EN
ÉN kibri-dit kibri-ditšá
u kaššapâtimeš šá u ai-ba-ti-šá

[80] e- ul in-ni-ip-pu-uš
e-bi-ši - ul iq-bi- -me
man-nu šá a-na kibri-dit ip-pu-šá kiš-pi
kibri-dit šá u êpušûmeš-niki-
-ru-ki ana-ku lu-ub-lut SU.EN

[85] ÉN kibri-dit ellitu šam-KUR.KUR šam-mu qud-du-šu ana-ku
Pure sulfur, *kurkur*-weed – I am the pure weed.
e-pi-šu-u-a apqallu šá apsî
My sorcerer is wise in the ways of the Deep [*usually given as "sea" or "ocean"*]
e-pi-iš-tu-u-a mârat da-nim šá šamêe
My sorceress is born of the daughter of the Sky-God ANU.
ki-i e-te-ni-ip-pu-šu-ni ul i-li-'-a-in-ni
Although they have bewitched me, they have not overwhelmed me.
ki-i e-pu-šu-si-na-a-ti iš-te-'u-si-na-a-ti
Since they have conjured sorcery and evil magick,

e-til-la-a kima nûnêmeš ina mêmeš-ia
Make them rise like a fish in my pond,
kîma šahi ina ru-šum-ti-ia
Like a pig in my sty,
kîma šam-maštakal ina ú-sal-li
Like a *matakal*-weed in my fields,
kîma šamsassati ina a-hi a-tap-pi
Like the reed-grass on the riverbank,
kîma zêr isuši ina a-hi tam-tim
Like a seed of the black tree on shoreline,

e-šá dillat-e e-šá dillat-e
[in all these] where my divine support exists, where my divine support exists,
nar-qa-ni a-na qaq-qa-ri
May you be emptied out onto the ground,
šá tu-na-sis-a-ni kim-mat-ku-nu ia-a-ši
You, who have shook your head at me!

ÉN dit qaqqadi-ia kibri-dit pa-da-at-ti
The god is my head, the sulfur is my [image]
šêpâ-ai na-a-ru šá man-ma la idûu ki-rib-šá
My feet are the river in whose depths no one knows.

šam-AN.HUL.LA pû-ia tâmtu ta-ma-ta rapaštumtum rit-ti
The *anhulla*-plant is my mouth, the sea of distant TIAMAT is my hand...

kîma dit qaqqadi-ia kibri-dit pa-da-at-ti
kîma <unreadable text in next 9 lines>
meš-ri-ti-ia-
-

[105] ÉN dit a-kul al-ti
ÉN e kaššapti-ia e-li-ni-ti-ia
- -ba-nu-uk-ki i-
- -šá šamêe parakki šá qaq-qa-ri
- -kibri-dit mârat ilimeš rabûtimeš

[110] -ki ina ûm bubbuli iptatar ru-hi-e-ki

ÉN at-ti tabtu šá ina áš-ri elli ib-ba-nu-ú
You are the salt that was formed in a the 'Pure Place'.
ana ma-ka-li-e ilimeš rabûtimeš i-šim-ki den-lil
A meal for the Great Gods, you have been fated by ENLIL;
ina ba-li-ki ul iš-šak-kan nap-tan ina é-kur
without you there is no meal in the E.KUR,
ina ba-li-ki ilu šarru BELU u rubû ul is-si-nu qut-rin-nu
without you, God, King and Master cannot smell the incense.

[115] ana-ku annanna apil annanna šá kiš-pi su-ub-bu-tu-in-ni
I, __ , son of __ have beheld the sorcery,
up-šá-še-e li-'-bu-in-ni
allowed the baneful plot to fester:
putri kiš-pi-ia tabtu pu-uš-ši-ri ru-hi-e-a
break the spells, salt! Dissolve the sorceries!

up-ša-še-e muh-ri-in-ni-ma kîma ili ba-ni-ia
Remove the baneful plan from me! Like unto my creator,
lul-tam-mar-ki
I will be free to give adoration!

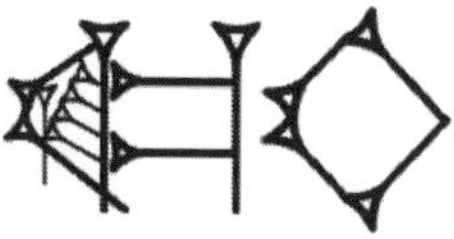

ÉN e kaššapti-ia lu rah-ha-ti-ia
[I laugh at you] my sorceress, medicine-man;
šá a-na bêriám ip-pu-hu išâta
who has lit the fires for one side,
a-na bêri iš-tap-pa-ra mâr šip-ri-ša
but sends her [watcher] to both sides,
ana-ku i-di-ma at-ta-kil ta-ka-lu
I know, I have strong conviction;
ina -ia ma-sar-tú ina bâbi-ia az-za-qap ki-din-nu
I have set a watcher in my house; at my gate, a protector,

ismaiâli-ia al-ta-me subâtú-li-in-na
I have enchanted a scarf to wrap around my bed,
ina rêš ismaiâli-ia a-za-raq šamnuhurtu
I have sprinkled *asadoetida* at the head of my bed,
dan-na-at šamnuhurtu-ma ú-na-ha-ra kal kiš-pi-ki
so the strong *asafoetida* fragrance will end all of your sorceries!

ÉN e kaššapti-ia lu rah-ha-ti-ia
šá a-na bêriam ippuhaha išâta

a-na bêri iš-tap-pa-ra mâr šip-ri-ša
ana-ku i-di-ma at-ta-kal ta-ka-la
ina- -ia ma-sar-tú ina bâbi-ia az-za-qap ki-din-nu
ina rêš ismaiâli-ia ašakan iššá-'-ir-ri
- -šá etimmi ri-hi-it GIRRA qa-mi-ki

ù dnisaba šar-ra-tu mu-ga-si-sa-at ubânatimeš-ki

ÉN e kaššapti-ia e-li-ni-ti-ia
My sorceress, [evil informant], I laugh at you,
šá tattallaki kal mâtâti
you, who blows back and forth over the lands,
ta-at-ta-nab-lak-ka-ti kal šadânimeš-ni
you, who crosses back and forth over the mountains,
ana-ku i-di-ma at-ta-kil ta-ka-lu
I know – and I have a firm conviction,

ina- -ia ma-sar-tú ina bâbi-ia az-za-qap ki-din-nu
in my house I have stationed a watcher, at the gate I put a protector;
ina imitti bâbi-ia u šumêli bâbi-ia
at the right of my gate and left of my gate

ul-te-iz-ziz LUGAL-gir-ra u dmis-lam-ta-è-a
I have set *lugal-girra* and *meslamtaea*;
ilimeš šá ma-sar-te na-si-ih lib-bi muš-te-mi-du kalâtimeš
may these 'guardian gods' burst the insides of the one who 'steals reason'!
kassaptuli-du-ku-ma ana-ku lu-ub-lut
May they kill the sorceress that I may live!

[145] ÉN e kaššapti-ia e-li-ni-ti-ia

šá tallakiki kal mâtâti
ta-at-ta-nab-lak-ka-ti kal šadânimeš-ni
ana-ku i-di-e-ma at-ta-kil ta-ka-lu
ina- -ia ma-sar-tú ina bâbi-ia az-zaqap
ki-din-nu

[150] <unreadable text throughout> ak -lu

ÉN rit-ti dman-za-ád .
(The first lines on the next tablet in the series.)

tuppu kam ma-aq-lu-ú
(Here ends the sixth tablet of the MAQLU.)

Tablet VII

ÉN rit-ti dman-za-ád GIR.TAB-meš
My hand is *manzad*, my scorpion;
ši-i kassaptuú-nak-ka-ma kiš-pi-šá
[she], the sorceress, gathers her spells,
ú- -pah-kim-ma ki-ma marrati ina šamêe
I [cover] you like the rainbow in the sky,
ú-za-qa-kim-ma kîma iltâni amurrî
I blow on you like the north-wind, the west-wind,

ú-sa-ap-pah urpata-ki ú-hal-laq ûm-ki
I destroy your clouds and dispel your bad weather!
ú-sap-pah kiš-pi-ki šá tak-ki-mi mu-šá u ur-ra
I destroy the sorcery you have gathered up both day and night,
ù na-áš-pa-rat zitarrutâa šá tal-tap-pa-ri ia-a-ši
and all malefic messages you send my way.
sa-lil nêbiru sa-lil ka-a-ru
NEBIRU [*boat of heaven's crossing*] calls, the harbor calls,
mârêmeš malâhi ka-li-šú-nu sal-lu
the sailors are resting all the while;

elî isdalti ù issikkuri na-du-u hur-gul-lu
the door and bolt are wrapped up,
na-da-at ši-pat-su-un šá dsiris u dnin-giš-zi-da
the incantations are laid down of SIDURI and NINGISZIDA,
šá lúkaššapi-ia u kaššapti-ia ip-šá bar-tum amât limuttimtim
the sorcery, the incantations, the evil speech, the evil word of my sorcerer and sorceress,

ai ithunimeš.ni ai i-ba-'-u-ni
should not come near; will not come in!
bâba ai êrubûnimeš.ni ana bîti
The door [gate] is barred; [they should not] enter the house!

[15] dnin-giš-zi-da li-is-suh-šú-nu-ti
NINGISZIDA, throw them out!
lib-bal-ki-tu-ma e-pi-šá-ti-šu-nu li-ba-ru
[May] they kneel down to catch their helpers!
ilu šarru BELU ù rubû lik-kil-mu-šú-nuina
[May] God, King and Master look at their evil unfavorably.
ina qâtê ili šarri BELI u rubî ai ú'si kaš-šap-ti
In [the] power of my God and king, the sorceress will not escape!
a-na-ku ina qí-bit MARDUK BEL nu-bat-ti
But I act in alignment with MARDUK, the Master of Magicians,

[20] ù dasari-lú-du BEL a-ši-pu-ti
MARDUK [*asariludu*], Master of the Incantations,
min-mu-ú e-pu-šu lu ku-ši-ru
may everything I have done here be successful!
ip-še te-pu-šá-ni li-sa-bil šâra
[May] the sorceries you have conjured against me turn into wind!

ÉN a-ra-hi-ka ra-ma-ni a-ra-hi-ka pag-ri
I sanctify you, my self; I sanctify you, the whole of my body;
ki-ma dsumuqân ir-hu-ú bu-ul-šú
like the *sumuqan* sanctifies his cattle,

[25] sênu im-mir-šá sabîtu ar-ma-šá atânu mu-ur-šá
the ewe with her lamb, the gazelle with her kid, the she-donkey with her foal,
isepinnu irsitimtim ir-hu-ú irsitimtim im-hu-ru zêr-šá
[like] the plow sanctifies the earth, and the earth receives [from the] plow, its seeds,
ad-di šipta a-na ra-ma-ni-ia
I have conjured an incantation upon myself!
li-ir-hi ra-ma-ni-ma li-še-se lum-nu
May it sanctify me and drive evil away!
ù kiš-pi ša zumri-ia li-is-su-hu
May they tear away the sorcery from my body,

[30] ilimeš rabûtimeš
the Great Gods!

ÉN šamnu ellu šamnu ib-bu šamnu nam-ru
Pure oil, clean [light] oil, shinning oil!
šamnu mu-lil zumri šá ilimeš
Oil [pure] which cleanses the gods!
šamnu mu-pa-áš-ši-ih širšir-a-na šá a-me-lu-ti
Oil which soothes the muscles of humans!

šaman šipti šá dé-a šaman šipti šá dasari-lú-du
Oil consecrated to the incantation of ENKI, oil of the incantation of MARDUK [*asariludu*]!

ú-ta-hi-id-ka šaman tap-šu-uh-ti
I have let you drip with the oil that cleanses
šá dé-a id-di-nu a-na pa-áš-ha-a-ti
that ENKI has given forth to heal [with].
ap-šu-uš-ka šaman balâti
I have rubbed you with the 'Oil of Life
ad-di-ka šipat dé-a BEL eri-du dnin-igi-kug
have placed you next to the incantation of ENKI, Lord of ERIDU and NINIGIKUG
at-ru-ud a-sak-ku ah-ha-zu
have chased away the *asakku* [the seizer],

šu-ru-up-pu-u ša zumri-ka
[the] chill is [removed] from your body.
ú-šat-bi qu-lu ku-ru ni-is-sa-tú šá pag-ri-ka
[I have] removed the frightful sound, the fear, the trembling of your body,
ú-pa-áš-ši-ih šir-a-ni mi-na-ti-ka la tâbâtimeš
[have] healed the tendons of your ailing members.
ina qí-bit dé-a šar apsî
Upon ENKI, Lord of the Deep,
ina tê ša dé-a ina šipat dasari-lú-du
with the formula of ENKI, [along] with the incantation of MARDUK [*asariludu*],

ina ri-kis ra-ba-bu šá dgu-la
[Clothed] in the 'large garments' of GULA,
ina qâtê pa-áš-ha-a-ti šá dnin-din-ug-ga
with the healing hands of NINDINUGGA,

ú dnin-a-ha-qud-du BEL šipti
and of NINAHAQUDDU, Master of Incantation,
ana annanna apil annanna šub-šu-ma dé-a šipat-ka šá balâti
let __, son of __ know, ENKI and you 'Incantation of Life'!
7 apqallê šu-ut eri-du li-pa-áš-ši-hu zumur-šu TU.EN
[May the] seven *apqallu* of Eridu heal his body!

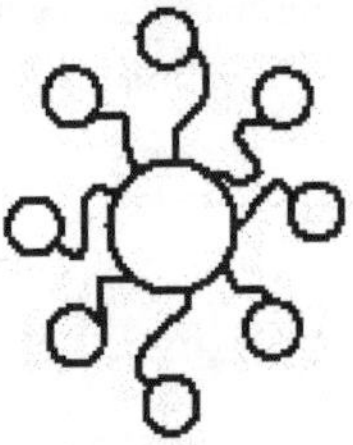

[50] ÉN den-lil qaqqadi-ia MULKAK.SI.ŠÁ la-a-ni
ENLIL is my head, the star *kaksisa* is my form;
pûtu SAMAS nap-hu
[the] forehead is SAMAS [*usually 'light of crescent'***],**
idâ-ai isgamlu šá bâb MARDUK
[my] arms [are] the curved sword of the Gate of MARDUK,
uzna-a-a li-'-u šêpâII-a-a lah-mu mu-kab-bi-sa-at lah-me
[my] ears are a (divine) tablet, my stomping feet [are a] snake.
at-tu-nu ilimeš rabûtimeš šá ina šamêe nap-ha-tu-nu
You, Great Gods, who are lit in the heavens,

[55] kîma an-na ku an- ip-šu bar-tum amât lemut-tim
Like the evil sorceries, spells and malediction
la itehhûmeš-ku-nu-ši la i-sa-ni-qú-ku-nu-ši
do not come near you, or even push up close,

ip-šû bar-tú amât lemut-tim la itehhû-ni la isanniqû-ni ia-šì ÉN
so may the baneful sorceries, spells and malediction not come near to me, or even push up close against me!

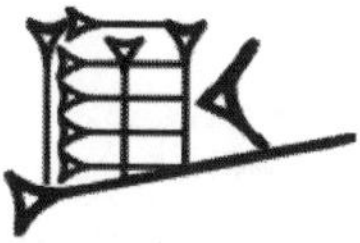

ÉN at-ti man-nu kassaptušá êpušušu sal-mi
Who are you, sorceress? You who has an [image] of me,
it-tu-lu la-a-ni êpušušu la-mas-si
who has observed my form and fashioned an [image],

i-mu-ru bal-ti ú-šar-ri-hu ga-ti
has seen my strength, has fashioned my [image],
ú-sab-bu-u nab-ni-tú
has studied the shape of my form,
ú-maš-ši-lu bu-un-na-ni-e-a
has reproduced [carefully] my features,
ub-bi-ru mi-na-ti-ia
has bound my appendages [members],
ú-kas-su-u meš-ri-ti-ia
has bound up my appendages [members],

ú-kan-ni-nu ma-na-ni-e-a
has distorted my nervous system;
ia-a-ši dé-a maš-maš ilimeš ú-ma-'-ra-an-ni
[but] ENKI, Enchanter of the Gods, has sent me;

ma-har SAMAS sa-lam-ki e-sir
in front of SAMAS I have drawn your [image].
la-an-ki ab-ni bal-ta-ki a-mur
I have drawn your [image]. I have observed your strength,
gat-ta-ki ú-šar-ri-ih nab-nit-ki ú-sab-bi
I have made your [image] and caught the shape of your form,

i-na dnisaba ellitimtim bu-un-na-an-ni-ki ú-maš-šil
I have duplicated your [image] using pure flour,
mi-na-ti-ki ub-bi-ir meš-ri-ti-ki ú-kas-si
I have bound your appendages; I have bound up your appendages,
ma-na-ni-ki ú-kan-ni-in
I have distorted your nervous system;
ip-šú te-pu-šin-ni e-pu-uš-ki
I have conjured on you the spell that you did cast on me.
mi-hir tu-šam-hir-in-ni ú-šam-hir-ki
I have let you have your evil encounter that you suffered me!

gi-mil tag-mil-in-ni ú-tir ag-mil-ki
I have let you have your revenge that you suffered me!
kiš-pi-ki ru-hi-ki ru-si-ki ip-še-te-ki lim-ni-e-te
Your sorcery, your spells, your evil, your malignance,
up-šá-še-ki ai-bu-te
your evil plans,
na-áš-pa-ra-ti-ki šá li-mut-ti
your evil messages,

râm-ki zêr-ki dipalû-ki zitarrutû-ki
[your] love, hate, imbalance and murder,

kadibbidû-ki dubbubu-ki li-kil-lu rêš-ki
[your] disease and calamities; may your head stop thinking!
it-ti mêmeš šá zumri-ia u mu-sa-a-ti šá qâtê-ia liš-šá-hi-it-ma
With [pure] water of my body, purifying water of my hands, may your evil be removed
a-na muh-hi-ki u la-ni-ki lil-lik-ma ana-ku lu-ub-lut
and fo to your head and form, that I may live!
e-ni-ta li-na-an-ni ma-hir-ta lim-hur-an-ni
May divine grace bless me and good fortune come to me!

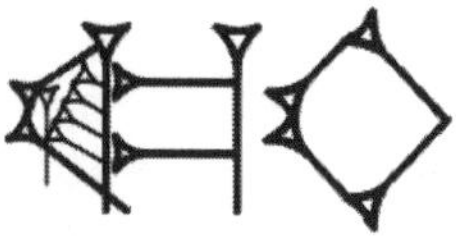

ÉN ba-'-ir-tú šá ba-'ra-a-ti
Catcher of catchers!

kassaptušá kaššapâtimeš
Sorceress of sorceresses!
šá ina sûqâtameš-ta na-da-tu še-is-sa
Who, in the streets, has spread their net,
ina ri-bit âli it-ta-na-al-la-ka ênâ-šá
whose eyes, dart about in the city square;
lúetlêmeš âli ub-ta-na-'
she targets the men in the city,

it-ti lúetlêmeš âli ub-ta-na-'-in-ni ia-a-ši
with the men of the city, she has targeted me [too].

ardâtimeš âli is-sa-na-hur
the girls of the city, she cavorts with,
it-ti ardâtimeš âli is-sa-na-hur-an-ni ia-a-ši
with the girls of the city, she cavorts with me [too].
e ú-ba-'-kim-ma lúkurgarêmeš lúeš-še-bi-e
I seek ... against you, *kur-garras* and *essebi*
rikis-ki a-hi-pi
I will break your bindings!
lúkaššapêmeš li-pu-su-ki rikis-ki a-hi-pi
May warlocks bewitch you, but I will break your bindings!

kaššapâtimeš li-pu-ša-ki rikis-ki a-hi-pi
May witches bewitch you, but I will break your bindings!
lúkurgarêmeš li-pu-šu-ki rikis-ki a-hi-pi
***Kurgarras* bewitch you, but I will break your bindings!**
lúeš-še-bu-ú li-pu-šu-ki rikis-ki a-hi-pi
***Essebu* bewitch you, but I will break your bindings!**
nar-šin-du-umeš li-pu-šu-ki rikis-ki a-hi-pi
***Narsindus* bewitch you, but I will break your bindings!**
mušlahhêmeš li-pu-šu-ki rikis-ki a-hi-pi
Snake-charmers bewitch you, but I will break your bindings!

a-gu-gil-lumeš li-pu-šu-ki rikis-ki a-hi-pi
***Agulgillu* bewitch you, but I will break your bindings!**

a-mah-has li-it-ki a-šal-la-pa lišân-ki
I devour your face. I rip out your tongue,
ú-ma-al-la ru-'-a-ta ênâII-ki
I fill your eyes with my spit,
ú-ša-lak a-hi-ki lil-lu-ta
I make your arms loose their strength [*literally "to become weak"***].**
ú ak-ka-a-ši ru-uq-bu-ta ú-ša-lak-ki
and for you to eat, I leave out rotten refuse,

[105] ù mimma ma-la te-te-ip-pu-ši ú-tar ana muh-hi-ki
and everything you have conjured against me, I turn back onto your head!

ÉN ep-ši-ki ep-še-ti-ki ep-še-et ep-ši-ki
Your enchantment and magick, the sorcery of your sorceress,
ep-še-et mu-up-pi-še-ti-ki
[the] sorcery of your sorcerer,
dé-a maš-maš ilimeš ú-pat-tir-ma mêmeš uš-ta-bil
ENKI, Father of Magicians, has undone [it all] and turned [it] to water!
pî-ki lim-nu e-pi-ra lim-la
May your evil mouth be filled with dirt from the earth!

[110] lišân-ki šá limuttimtim ina qí-e lik-ka-sir
May your evil tongue be tied up with a string!
ina qí-bit den-bi-lu-lu BEL balâti TU.EN
[All this] by the decree of *Enbilulu*, Master of Life!

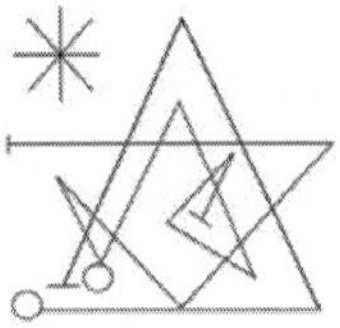

ÉN ki-is-ri-ki ku-us-su-ru-ti
Your bound knots,
ip-še-ti-ki lim-ni-eti up-šá-še-ki ai-bu-ti
your evil spells and evil manifestations,
na-áš-pa-ra-tu-ki šá limuttimtim
your evil intentions spoken,

[115] dasari-lú-du maš-maš ilimeš ú-pat-tir-ma ú-šá-bil sara
MARDUK [*asariludu*], Master of Magicians, has done and removed [all of this]!
pî-ki lim-nu epirahi.a lim-ma-li
May your evil mouth be filled up with dirt from the earth,
lišan-ki šá limuttimtim ina qí-e lik-ka-sir
and may your evil tongue be tied up with a string!
ina qí-bit den-bi-lu-lu BEL balâti TU.EN
[All this] by the decree of *Enbilulu*, Master of Life!

ÉN am-si qa-ti-ia ub-bi-ba zu-um-ri
I have washed my hands; I have purified my body

ina mêmeš naqbi ellûtimeš šá ina eri-du ib-ba-nu-u
in [pure] waters which come from Eridu proper;
mimma lim-nu mimma lâ tâbu
may all diseased spirits, all of the evil spirits and misfortune
šá ina zumri-ia šêrêmeš-ia šir'ânêmeš-ia bašûu
that in my body, my form and my being exists,
lumun šunâtimeš idâtimeš ittâtimeš limnêtimeš lâ tâbâtimeš
anxiety by way of evil and unfavorable dreams, harbingers of doom,
lumun šîrîmeš ha-tu-ti par-du-ti lemnû-timeš lâ tâbûtimeš
anxiety by way of false dreams, evil visions and misfortune,

lipit qâti hi-niq šu'i ni-iq ni-qi nêpeš-ti barû-ti
by laying-of-hands, strangulation of life, of divination,
šá at-ta-ta-lu u-me-šam
by all of that which I see every day,

ú-kab-bi-su ina sûqi e-tam-ma-ru ina a-ha-a-ti
and that which I step upon in the street and what I see around me,
še-ed lem-utti ú-tuk-ku lim-nu
the evil *sedu*, the evil *utukku*,
mursu di-'di-lip-ta
illness, headache, upset,

qu-lu ku-ru ni-is-sa-tú ni-ziq-tú im-tu-uta-ni-hu
terror, fear, quivering, worry, depression, apathy,
'ú-a a-a hu-su-su qis lib-bi
pains, aches, cramps, leprosy,
gi-lit-tum pi-rit-tum a-dir-tum
more fear, obsession, terror,
ár-rat ilimeš mi-hir-ti ilimeš ta-zi-im-ti
sin, the unfavorably hand and wrath of Gods,
ni-iš ilî ni-iš ilî ni-iš qâti ma-mit
curses born of oaths to God and the oath-swearing raised hand,

lum-nu kiš-pi ru-hi-e ru-si-e up-šá-še-e lem-nu-ti šá amêlûtimeš
sorcery, spells, evil manifestations of humans,
it-ti mêmeš šá zumri-ia u mu-sa-a-ti šá qâte-ia
may they all, with the clean water of my body and hands,
liš-šá-hi-it-ma ana muhhi salam nig-sagilêe lil-lik
be sent to the deceiver whose [image] is before me!
salam nigsagilêe ár-ni di-na-ni li-iz-bil
May my sin carry my [image] instead of me!
su-ú-qu ù su-lu-ú li-pat-ti-ru ár-ni-ia
May the causeway and path cleanse me of the sin!

[140] e-ni-tum li-na-ni ma-hir-tum lim-hur-an-ni
May the grace [of the highest] bless me, may favorable conditions come to me!
am-hur mi-ih-ru lim-hu-ru-in-ni
I have lived through [this] experience [enough]; may it now turn favorably toward me!
u-mu šul-ma arhu hi-du-ti šattu hagalla-šá li-bil-la
May the day bring health, the month bring joy and the year its prosperity.
dé-a SAMAS u MARDUK ia-a-ši ru-sa-nim-ma
ENKI, SAMAS and MARDUK come to my aid!
lip-pa-áš-ru kiš-pu ru-hu-u ru-su-u
May the evil sorcery, the evil spells, all be dissolved [to nothingness]!

[145] up-šá-šu-ú lim-nu-ti šá a-me-lu-ti
May the evil manifestations of men and the *ù ma-mit lit-ta-si šá zumri-ia*
baneful oath sword all now leave my body!

ÉN te-bi še-e-ru mesâa qâte-ia
Dawn is coming forth, my hands are washed;
-ma qaq-qa-ru mu-hur up-ni-ia
[my iniquity] is cleansed, my sin is absolved.
šá kassaptuú-kaš-šip-an-ni
Because the sorceress has enchanted me,

eš-še-bu ú-sa-li-'-an-ni
the wicked witch has made me sick,
SAMAS pi-šir-ta li-bil-am-ma
SAMAS, I call on you to bring me salvation!
irsitimtim lim-hur-an-ni
May the earth protect me!

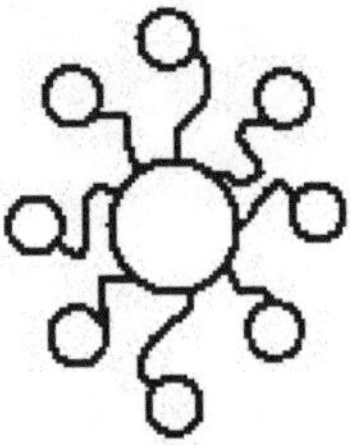

ÉN it-tam-ra še-e-ru pu-ut-ta-a dalati
Dawn has come forth; the doors have opened;
a-lik ur-hi it-ta-si abulla
the traveler has passed through [the gate];

mâr šipri is-sa-bat har-ra-na
the messenger has taken to the road.
e-piš-tum e te-pu-šin-ni
Witch, hey, did you try to bewitch me?
ra-hi-tum e tu-ri-hi-in-ni
Enchantress, hey, did you try to enchant me?
ú-tal-lil ina na-pa-ah dšamši
[Well], now I am freed with the radiant light of the rising sun;
mimma ma-la te-pu-ši ù tu-uš-te-pu-ši
Whatever witchcraft you believe you have done,

li-tir-ru-ma li-is-ba-tu-ki ka-a-ši
may it all turn back upon you – yes, you!

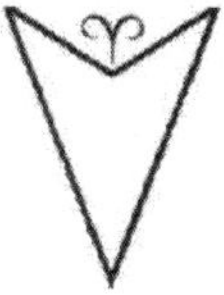

ÉN še-ru-um-ma še-e-ru
Morning, [glorious] morning!
an-nu-ú šá lúkaššapi-ia u kaššapti-ia
[Honestly] my sorcerer and sorceress
it-bu-nim-ma kîma mârêmeš lúnâri ú-lap-pa-tú nu-'-šú-nu
have plucked at their cords like minstrels.
ina bâbi-ia iz-za-zi PALIL
At my gate stands PALIL,

ina rêš ismaiâli-ia iz-za-zi LUGAL-edin-na
at the head of my bed guards *Lugal-edinna*,
a-šap-pa-rak-kim-ma šá bâbi-ia PALIL
I send you from my gate, PALIL;
šá rêš ismaiâli-ia LUGAL-edin-na
and from my bed, *Lugal-edinna*.
mîli bêri dib-bi-ki mîli har-ra-ni a-ma-ti-ki
Your speech will turn around on you [like a] flood on the streets,
ú-tar-ru kiš-pi-ki ru-hi-ki ú-sa-ab-ba-tu-ki ka-a-ši TU.EN
your sorceries, charms and spells will [come back] to seize you, yes you!

ÉN ina še-rì misâa qâtâ-ai
In dawn-time, my hands have been cleansed,
šur-ru-ú dam-qu li-šar-ra-an-ni
may a prosperous beginning start for me;
tu-ub lìb-bi tûbub šêri li-ir-te-da-an-ni
may happiness and good fortune ever follow alongside me,
e-ma ú-sa-am-ma-ru su-um-mi-ra-ti-ia lu-uk-šu-ud
whatever it is that I desire, may I obtain my desires,
šunât e-mu-ru ana damiqtimtim liš-šak-na
whenever I dream, may those be favorable,

ai ithâa ai isniq mimma lim-nu mimma lâ tâbu
and [keep away] anything evil, anything malevolent,
ru-hi-e šá lúkaššapi u kaššapti
any evil enchantment of the sorcerer and sorceress,
ina qí-bit dé-a SAMAS u MARDUK u ru-bâti BELIT i-li TU.EN
by the decree of ENKI, SAMAS, MARDUK and the Queen, Lady of the Gods [of the heavens]!

ÉN am-si qâtê-ia am-te-si qâtê-ia
- -hu-u mêmeš mîli ra-šub-bat nâri

<unreadable text> bi-li bal-ta-ki
- -NI LUM mi-ra-ni ra-šub-bat-ku-nu
kîma mêmeš an-nu-ti ip-šú bar-tum amât limuttimtim
lâ itehûu lâ i-qar-ri-bu
ip-šú bartu amât limuttimtim lâ itehâ

[185] lâ i-qar-ri-ba ia-a-ši SU.EN-É-NU-RU

ÉN a-di tap-pu-ha ú-qa-a-ka be-lí SAMAS
(The opening line o f the next tablet in the series.)

tuppu kam ma-aq-lu-ú
(Here ends the [seventh] tablet of the MAQLU.)

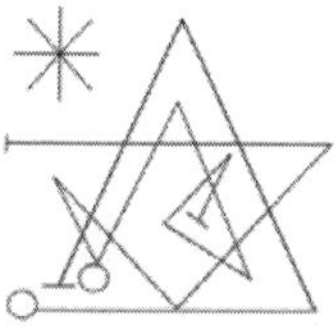

Tablet VIII

ÉN a-di tap-pu-ha ú-qa-a-ka be-lí SAMAS
<unreadable text throughout tablet> šá-qa-a ri-šá-ai
- be-lí SAMAS
- tap-ta-šar a-... la
-

[5] - it-te-bi ši-kar-šá
- -te-bu-u ar-qu-šá
ú-ma-'-ra-an-ni be-lí SAMAS
- -e-pu-šá-an-ni
- -ú-ra-ah-ha-an-ni

[10] - -šá a-hu-la-ai
- -a-hi nâridiqlat
- -a-tap-pi

- -na-a-ru
- -u

-
ÉN it-tap-ha SAMAS a-kaš-šad
ú-na-a -
ú-še-li -
e-piš-tú -

gallû id- -
- -šu-lu -
- -te-ih- -
pa- -
be- -

dé-a -
dnin- -
za-am- -
šá la -
kal a-ma-tu-šá -

li-ra- -
pi- -
-

ÉN un-du kassaptui-bir nâra
After the sorceress has crossed the river,
- -u iš-la-a -
she escaped me by going under the Deep.

e-piš-ti áš-bat ina ni-bi-ri
My sorceress sits lonely in NI.BI.RI
- -šu-uš ka-a-ri
[My sorceress sits lonely] on the shore.
ub-ta-na-'-an-ni ia-ši ana sa-ha-li-ia
She still seeks me, seeks her revenge.
li- -ši-ma apqallêmeš šá apsî
May the *apqalle* of the Deep go to her,
- -zi ni-me-qí ni-kil-ti dea iq-bu-u la-pan-šá
[let her taste] the clever wisdom of ENKI, King of the Deep!

dé-a šar apsî lih-da-a pa-ni-šá
May you rejoice with ENKI, King of the Deep!
li-sa-hi-ip-ši be-en-na te-šá-a ra-i-ba
May [my] paralysis and anger be subsided,
li-tir hur-ba-as-sa
[my] fear be removed,
- -pu-luh-ta šá i-da-a eli-šá
[I have held] fear against you,
ana elî salmânimeš-šá misâa qâtâ-ia
[but now] I wash my hands over their [images],

i-na riqqukukri šá šadî riqquburâši elli
with *chicory*, pine and cypress;
i-na šam-DIL.BAT mu-ul-lil amêli misâa qâtâ-ia
with the *dilbat*-weed that cleanses humans, I have washed my hands.

e-te-lil ana-ku -ina elî sêri-šá
pure I have become [like the water] more than she can,
kiš-pu-šá lim-lu-u- sêru
Her sorceries, in the desert [may they rot].
amâtemeš-šá šâru- lit-bal
I carry away her words [to the wind]

[50] ù mimma ma-la e-pu-šu li-tur ana šâri
and every enchantment she has manifested, I throw to the wind!

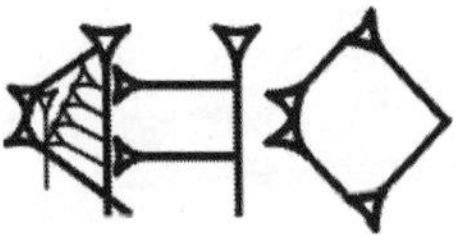

ÉN ultu dsumuqân ina šadî ilsûú da-la-la
After *Sumuqan* had begun the victory song on the moutnain;
ultu kal i-lu-ú a-na na-kas isbîni
and everyone had ascended to cut *tamarisk*;
áš-bat-ma ummu - -šú
the mother and father sat down.
áš-bu-ma i-ma-li-ku- ahu -
they convene to counsel the bother and sister.

[55] at-ti man-nu kassaptušá ia-a-ši u ram-ni-ia
Whoever you are, sorceress, who I have now bewitched,
e-piš-tú e-pu-šá kiš-pi ik-ši-pu
Witch who has bewitched [and who I have now bewitched],

kiš-pu-šá lu-u šâru kiš-pu-šá lu-u me-hu-ú
may your spells be wind, may your spells be lost in a storm,
kiš-pu-šá lu-u pu-u lit-tap-ra-šá-du elî-šá
may your spells be grains of dust that fly up in your face!

ÉN an-nu-u e-nin-na-ma

kassaptunak-rat-an-ni
ù muš-te-piš-tú na-bal-ku-ta-at-an-ni
- -ina kiš-pi-šá
- -kaš-šap-tú
- -ka-su-ti

- -lib-bi-šá
- -šipat-ki
- -amât limuttimtim-ki
- -dé-a -ka- -na a-na - uš-te-pí-lu-ki- dé-a BEL -
ù mimma ma-la te-pu-ši

li-šam-hir-ki ka-a-ši SU.EN
ÉN pu-u id-bu-ub lim-na-a-ti
pu-u im-ta-lik-si-na-ti
šá kaš-šap-a-ti kiš-pi-ši-na
šá eš-še-ba-a-ti ši- -ši-na-ti

li-šab-ri-ši-na-ti
li-šal-lu-ši-na-ti
ina ši-pat - ZI pû lišânu
na-áš-pa-rat mûši u kal ûmimi
šá - te-pu-šá-ni ia-a-ši

tal- -pa-ra-ni ana ram-ni-ia - kiš-pi-ku-nu u ku-šá-pi-

ku-nu-kîma mêmeš mu- sa-a-ti a-sur-ra-a li-mal-li
ÉN e-piš-tu muš-te-piš-tú mu-ri-bat kiš-pi ru-hi-e - -ri mu--
-napištim ta-bi-kát - -ki- SAG.DU -
-ta-pi- -
- -SAMAS ku-
- -irsitimtim ai ú-še- -

[85] ana lúpagri-ki našru u zibu li-in-na-ad-ru
...[and may] eagles and vultures scour your dead body!
qu-lu hur-ba-šu lim-qu-ut elî-ki
Pain and fear, may it befall you!
kalbu u kalbatu li-ba-as-si-ru-ki
Hound and bitch, may they tear you apart!
kalbu u kalbatu li-ba-as-si-ru šêrêmeš-ki
Hound and bitch, may they tear your flesh away!
ina qí-bit dé-a SAMAS u MARDUK u rubâti dmah TU.EN
By the decree of ENKI, SAMAS, MARDUK and the goddess MAH!

ÉN at-ta silli at-ta ba-aš-ti
You are my strength [like] a shield;
at-ta dšêdi at-ta ga-at-ti
You are the 'guardian god' of my form,
at-ta pa-da-at-ti at-ta du-u-ti
You are my [image], my barrier [wall],
- -tae
. . .
e tam-hur kiš-pi e tam-hur ú-pi-ši
Hey, spell-crafter! Hey, evil-doer! You are finished!

KI.MINA šag-gaš-tú KI.MINA na-kas napištimtim
The same for a murderess, the same for the remover of life,
KI.MINA ru-'-ut-ta -ab-tu
the same for friendship-breakers,
KI.MINA kadibbidâ KI.MINA dipa-lâa
the same for the seizing disease, the same for the worldly injustice,
KI.MINA zêru KI.MINA ši- -pi-ši
the same for hate, the same for [violence],
limnûtimeš - -ti
[the same for all of the] evils of the [world].

at-ta ia-ú a-na-ku ku-ú
Great God, you are mine and I am yours,
man-ma-an ai il-mad-ka mimma lim-nu ai ithi-ka
may none but me counsel with you, may evil never come close to you,
ina qí-bit dé-a SAMAS MARDUK
by the decree of ENKI, SAMAS, MARDUK
u frubâti dmah TU.EN
and the Queen, MAH!

tuppu kam ma-aq-lu-ú
(*Here ends the [eighth] tablet of the MAQLU.*)

Tablet IX*

e-nu-ma ni-pi-še šá ma-qa-lu-u te-ip-pu-šu
<unreadable text in next 20 lines> -
ÉN al-si-ku-nu-ši- -e
- -bi-šú -ma

[5] - -salam lipî
- -taškan-ma
- -in-na-at-tuk
- -a-di
- -hu-lu-up-paq-qi

* Translation Note: Very unfortunately, the final tablet of the MAQLU series, also known as the 'ceremonial tablet' is mostly destroyed. This tablet confers important 'ritual information' to the priest-magician conducting the rites. Great effort has been used based on the fragments still available to paraphrase the text, a combined effort between editor and translator for this edition!

- -mashatu
- -tâbti tašakan
- -tu
- -šiptu šú tamannu-ma
- -hu-lu-up-pa-qi

- -tú
- -ki-tum - -meš
- -u tam-
- -tú u mashatu
- -ti- -

- -is-
- -salam itti salam titi
- -hu-lu-paq-qi
- -ina elî gizilâ tašakanan-ma
- -hu tata-ras-ma tamannunu

[Paraphrase: "when you perform the rites of the MAQLU tablet series" follow the following methods: When using the incantations that describe an object, have a representation of that object; when defacing the material images, follow a like-is-like preference: so a figure of salt can be crushed, of dough can be 'eaten' or 'devoured', an image made of wax should be held over a fire until the wax drips – all following in correlation with the series-texts. If necessary, the incantations may each be recited three times during their cycle; but be sure to follow the prescribed chronology (sequence) of the series: since there is an intentional purpose behind the MAQLU being given as it is from 'Babylonian' sources that venerate ENKI and MARDUK.**]**

[25] qanû tâbu ina libbi tu-sa-an-na-aš sa-lam dakî
ina išât kibri-it ta-qal-lu asu MUK
isata ana libbi hu-lu-up-paq-qi tanaddi

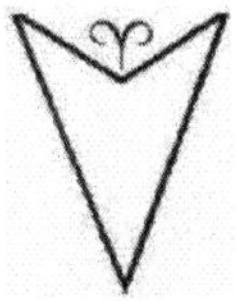

Materials to fashion the images

ÉN NUSKU šur-bu-u ma-lik ilîmeš rabûtimeš salam lipî
"Glorious NUSKU, Counsellor of the Gods..." – an image of *talcum*.
ÉN GIRRA BELu git-ma-lu gaš-ra-a-ta na-bi šum-ka salam siparri kibri-dit
"GIRRA, lord and master, perfect and powerful..." – an image of *copper* or *sulfur*.

[30] ÉN GIRRA a-ri-ru bu-kur da-nim salam siparri
"GIRRA, born of ANU..." – an image of *copper*.
ÉN GIRRA a-ri-ru mar a-nim salam lîši
"GIRRA, raging fire born of ANU..." – an image of *dough*.
ÉN GIRRA gaš-ru u-mu na-an-du-ru salam titi
"GIRRA, bringer of terrible storms..." – an image of *clay*.
ÉN GIRRA šar-hu bu-kur da-nim salam itti
"GIRRA, powerful son of ANU..." – an image of *asphalt*.
ÉN ki-eš libeš ki-di-eš salam kuspi
"*kes libes kides...*" – an image of *sesame-butter*.

<u>***Materials to fashion the images (continued)***</u>

[35] ÉN e-pu-šú-ni etenippušûnimeš.ni salam itti šá gassa bullulu

"They have bewitched me, they have hexed..." - an image of *asphalt* covered with *plaster*.

ÉN at-ti man-nu kassaptušá ina nâri im-lu-' tîta-ai

"Whoever you are, sorceress, who gathers clay..."

salam titi šá lipâ bullulu

- an image of *clay* covered with *talcum* [salt, powder].

ÉN at-ti man-nu kassaptušá tub-ta-na-in-ni

"Whoever you are, sorceress, who visits me unceasingly..."

salam isbîni salam iserini

- an image *tamarisk*-wood and/or one of *cedar*.

[40] ÉN kaššaptum mut-tal-lik-tum šá sûqâ-timeš salam tîti

"Sorceress who wanders the streets..." - an image of *clay*.

lipû ina rêš lib-bi-sa êra ina kalâtimeš-šá tu-sa-na-áš

(You put the *talcum* on the stomach [of the image] and stuff her kidneys with wood.)

ÉN ta ši-na mârâtimeš da-nim šá šamêe salam lipî hi-im-ma-ti

"Two are the daughters of the Sky-God ANU..." - an image of *talcum* and *garbage* [refuse].

ÉN kassaptunir-ta-ni-tum salam dakî

"Sorceress, murderess..." - an image of *wax*.

ÉN dit ellu nam-ru qud-du-šú ana-ku salam itti

"I am the light, pure and shinning..." - an image of *asphalt*.

Materials to fashion the images (continued)

[45] ÉN la-man-ni su-tu-ú e-la-mu-ú ri-da-ni
"The man from the SUTI-tribe sees me, the ELAMITE chases me..."
salam itti šá kibri-dit
– an image of *asphalt* next to one of *sulfur*.
ÉN at-ti man-nu kassaptušá iq-bu-u a-mat limuttimtim-ia ina libbi-šá
"Who are you, evil sorceress, in whose heart the evil spell against me resides..."
salam titi ina kunukki arqi amâta-šá ta-šá-tar
– an image of *clay* (you should write the 'word' on a green cylinder-seal).
ÉN at-ti ia-e šá te-pu-šin-ni ISTAR - -
"You, who has betwitched my goddess..."

[50] ha-ha-a šá ú-tu-ni um-me-en-na šá di-qa-ra
– an image using clumps of *ash* from the furnace, and *soot* clinging to the pots.
ina mêmeš ta-mah-ha-ah-ma ana qaqqad salam titi ta-tab-bak
(You mix it with water and pour it over the head of your *clay* image.)
ÉN šá e-pi-šá-an-ni ul-te-piš-an-ni maqur titi
"She was has bewitched me..." – use the [image] in a ship or *boat of clay*
2 salmu ina libbi
with two figures inside.
ÉN maqurri-ia NANNA-SIN ú-še-piš
"My boat, NANNA-SIN possesses..." – an image

Materials to fashion the images (continued)

[55] - -salam lîšiÉN
... of *dough*.
LA sûqâtimeš am-me-ni tug-tan-na-ri-en-ni
LA sûqi ir-bit-ti lipa tapaššaš nabâsa ta-ka-rik
ÉN rit-tu-um-ma rit-tum rit-ta lipî
"Hand! Hand..." – an image of a *hand*, made of *talcum*.
ÉN rit-tum-ma rit-tum <unreadable text>

[60] ÉN biš-li biš-li bal-lu-ur-ta qanêmeš šá gi-sal-li
"Boil! Boil..." – an image and a *cross* made of *pipes of reed*.
2 qanâtimeš šá ma-lu-ú ina muh-hi a-ha-meš ta-par-rik
(Two pipes are filled with blood and exfrement, lay them in a 'cross' pattern
ina ni-ri ina qabal -
in the middle of [*presumably "your magick circle"*].
2 salam lipi 2 salam -
Two figures of *talcum* and two figures of ...
ina ap-pa-a-ta šá bal-lu-ur-ta te-en-ni-ma
place these at the four points of the cross.)

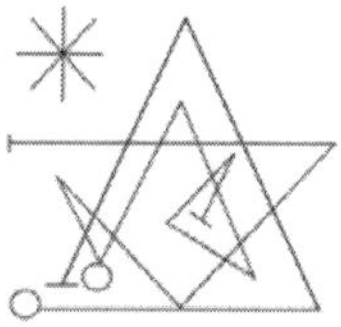

[65] tašakanan- <unreadable text in next 15 lines>

Materials to fashion the images (continued)

ÉN at-ta man-nu kassaptušá zitarrutâa êpušuš
"Whoever you are, sorceress, who has committed murder..."
hu-sab- -
– an image using three branches...
ÉN nir-ti-ia kaššapti-ia u ku-šá-pa-ti-ia
"My murderess, my sorceress and the 'greater' sorceress..."
lipû uban titi- -
– an image of *talcum*...

[70] ÉN šá dšamšiši man-nu abu-šú
"Who is the father of the sun-god..."
markas šipâti pisâti riksê ta-rak-kas
– an image with a white piece of *wool* tied in three *knots*.
ÉN i-pu-šá-ni i-te-ni-ip-pu-šá-ni
"I am being bewitched..."
markas šipâti pisâti riksê ta-rak-kas
– an image with a white piece of *wool* tied in seven *knots*.

ÉN ru-ú-a kaš-ša-pat ana-ku pa-ši-rak
<unreadable text throughout>

[75] LA-ta sûqi irbitti ta- -
ÉN e-piš-ta ù muš-te-piš-ta ri- -
ÉN man-nu pû ip-til pû- -
ÉN du-un-na-ni du-un-na-ni
ta-bi-lu ka- -

Materials to fashion the images (continued)

ÉN at-ti man-nu kassaptušá te-te-ni-ip-pu-šá
"Whoever you are, sorceress, you who unceasingly enchants..."
riqqukukru šamhašûtu ù pû ta-šar-rap
– burn the image with *chicory, thyme* and granules *of grain*.
ÉN zêru ša te-pu-šá-ni tu-še-pi-šá-ni ana muh-hi-ku-nu
ÉN at-ta man-nu kassaptušá ki-ma šûti ik-ki-mu ûmi kam
ÉN šá-ru-uh la-a-ni KI.MINA

ÉN šir'ane tu-qas-si-ra
ÉN at-tu-nu mêmeš ina mêmeš tu-na-ah
ÉN e-piš-ú-a e-piš-tu-u-a ina mêmeš tu-na-ah
ÉN iz-zi-tu-nu šam-ra-tu-nu ina mêmeš tu-na-ah
ÉN ak-bu-us gallâ-ai <unreadable text in next 5 lines>

ÉN hu-la zu-ba ina niqnaqqi šá pân NUSKU- -
ÉN šadûu lik-tùm-ku-nu-šú
aban šadîi ina muh-hi niqnaqqi tašak-kanan
ÉN i-sa-a i-sa-a tamannunu
mashata tanaddidi- -

arki-su ÉN UDUG HUL EDIN.NA.ZU.ŠE a-di ni-pi-ši-ša
...thereafter, recite the incantation: "Evil demon, to your desert..." to the outer threshold;
tamannu-ma mashata bâbâtime te-sir
[then] encircle the entrance-ways with blessed [pure] flour.
a-na bîti terrub-ma a-šar ma-aq-la-a taq-lu-u a-meš ŠUB.ŠUB.DI
Return to the house – the place where you have performed the MAQLU – libate with water.

Materials to fashion the images (continued)

ÉN a-nam-di šipta a-na pu-uh-ri ilîmeš ka-la-a-ma tamannunu
"I cast an incantation upon the assembly of All the Gods."
ÉN den-lil qaqqadi-ia pa-nu-ú-a u-mu- -
"ENLIL is my head, I rise to face the day..."

[100] ÉN e-piš-ta qu-um-qu-um-ma-ta riqqukuk-ru
"The sorceress is a *qumqummatu...*" – an image with *chicory*.
ÉN riqqukukru-ma riqqukukru pû di-iq-me-en-na
ÉN riqqukikru-ma riqqukukru - -riqqukukru
ÉN e kaššapti-ia e-li-ni-ti-ia riqqukukru
"Hey, my sorceress, my nightmare..." – use *chicory*.
ÉN la-am dnin-gir-su ina šadî il-su ú da-la-a riqqukukru
"In front of NINGIRSU..." – use *chicory*.

[105] ÉN e kassaptuú-kaš-šip-an-ni riqqukukru
"The sorceress has bewitched..." – use *chicory*
lipû lu-ba-ri-e parsûtimeš
also *talcum* and cut pieces of *clothing*.
ÉN at-ta e šá êpušuš ka-la-ma riqqukukru
ÉN kibri-dít ellitimtim mârat šamêe ra-bûtimeš ana-ku kibri-dít

[110] ÉN kibri-dít kibri-dít - -dít kibri-dít
"Sulfur. Sulfur..." – use *sulfur*.
ÉN kibri-dít ellitutu šam-KUR.KUR šam-mu qud-du-šú ana-ku
kibri-dít šam-KUR.KUR
ÉN dít qaqqadi-ia kibri-dít pa-da-at-ti
kibri-dít šamAN.HUL.LA šamimhur-lim

Materials to fashion the images (continued)

ÉN dít a-kul al-ti kibri-dít
ÉN e kaššapti-ia e-li-ni-ti-ia
idêe ul ide kibri-dít
ÉN at-ti tabtu šá ina aš-ri elli ib-ba-nu-u
ana elî kurban tâbti tamannunu-ma

ina elî niqnaqqi šá qu-ta-ri šá ina rêš ismaiâli tašakanan
ÉN e kaššapti-ia lu rah-hat-ia
ana elî šamnuhurti tamannunu-ma
ina elî niqnaqqi šá ina rêš ismaiâli taša-kanan
subâtú-li-in-na ismaiala taltamimi

ÉN e kaššapti-ia lu rah-hat-ia
ana elî iššá-ir-ri tamannunu-ma
ina elî niqnaqqi šá ina rêš ismaiâli ta-šakanan
ÉN e kaššapti-ia e-li-ni-ti-ia šá tattana-laki ka-lu mâtâtimeš
a-na elî hu-sab êri tamannunu-ma

[Paraphrase: Working through the list of incantations found throughout the MAQLU, the ritual tablet describes the presence of an herb a stone or an image such as it already appears within the text of the incantation.**]**

ina imitti bâbi u šumêli bâbi kamîi ta-šakanan
ÉN e kaššapti-ia e-li-ni-ti-ia
ana elî aban šadîi tamannunu-ma
ina tarbasi ta-na-suk
qu-ta-ri šá ÉN den-lil qaqqadi-ia

ma-la ana riksêmeš šat-ru

Materials to fashion the images (continued)

ištenišmeš tuballal-ma tu-qat-tar-šú
ÉN den-lil qaqqadi-ia tamannunu
ÉN rit-ti dman-za-ád mashatu u bil-litu
a-na rikis lúmarsi taballal-ma

šamnu tâbu sip-pi-e bâbânimeš taltappat
ÉN a-ra-ah-hi ra-ma-ni GAR šamni
ÉN šamnu ellu šamu ib-bu GAR šamni
ÉN den-lil qaqqadi-ia muKAK.SI.ŠÁ la-a-ni
šipâtimeš an-na-a-ti ŠID-nu-ma- -

Ì.GIŠ ka-la UZU.MEŠ-šú ŠÉŠ- -
ÉN ENŠADA DUMU.UŠ ÉKUR šá te-ret DINGIR.MEŠ GAL.MEŠ
ENŠADA LUGAL šu-te-šir KASKAL-ka-ana- -
arki-šú ZÌ.SUR.RA-a GIŠ.NÁ te-es-sir
ÉN SAG.BA SAG.BA ÉN tùm-mu-ú bîtu

i-na še-ri - -pa šur-pu ta-šar-rap
šur-pu- - bâba tušessi-ma taarki-
šú ÉN at-ti man-nu kassaptušá êpušu sal-mi tamannunu
salam kaššapti šá qêmi ina libbi erûnam-si-e te-is-sir
salam titi šá kaššapti ana elî tašakanan qâtê-šú ana elî imisisi

ÉN ba-'-ir-tú šá ba-'-ra-a-ti
salam lúkaššapi u kaššapti
šá qêmi ina libbi erûnam-si-e te-is-sir
salam titi šá lúkaššapi u kaššapti ina elî salam qêmi tašakanan
qâtê-šú ina elî imisisi ina hu-sab êri ana šú i-kar-rit

Materials to fashion the images (continued)

ÉN ip-ši-ki ip-še-te-ki mis qâtê
ÉN kisrêmeš-ki kussurûtimeš mis qâtê eprah-ia
ana libbi erûnam-si-e ta-na-suk
ÉN am-si qâtê-ia ub-ba-ab zumri-ia
ana eli salam pûhi qâtê-šú imisisi

ÉN te-bi še-e-ru mis qâtê
ÉN it-tam-ra še-e-ru mis qâtê
ÉN še-ru-um-ma še-e-ru mis qâtê
ÉN ina še-rì misâa qâtII-ai mis qâtê
ÉN am-si qâtê-ia am-te-si qâtê-ia mis qâtê

ÉN a-di tap-pu-ha isbinu šam-DIL.BAT aban suluppi
pû gassu unuq abanšubi riqqukukru
riqquburâšu qâtê-šú imisisi
ÉN it-tap-ha SAMAS a-bi mâti mis qâtê
ÉN un-du kassaptui-bir nâra mis qâtê

[Paraphrase: Numerous lines appear here that match with the openings of various incantations in the later part of the MAQLU series. All of them denote "*handwashing*" as the ritual action, or else the sprinkling of blessed waters.**]**

ÉN ultu dsumuqân ina šadî ilsûú da-la-la
pû ana libbi karpatLA.SAR tanaddidi-ma
ina pî-šú ana libbi nam-si-e tanappahah
ÉN an-nu-u in-nin-na-ma
salam kaššapti šá titi teppušuš-ma aban šadî ina rêš libbi-šá-tašakanan

qâtê-šú ana muh-hi imisisi
ina hu-sab êri ana šú i-kar-rit
ÉN pu-ú id-bu-ub lim-na-a-ti mis qâtê

Materials to fashion the images (continued)

ÉN e-piš-ti muš-te-piš-ti ina mu-ri-bat kiš-pi ru-hi-e
akâlêh-ia ta-ám salam lúkaššapi u kaššapti

[185] šá lîši teppušuš-ma ina libbi akâlêhi.a tarakkas-ma
ina imitti-šú u šumêli-šú tanašši-ma šipta tamannunu-ma
a-na kalbi u kalbati ta-nam-din
ÉN at-ta silli mêmeš karpatpursîtu tumalli-ma
- -ina libbi ŠI-ma

[190] - -liš tušessi tasallah
arki-šú ÉN anaššiši gam-li-ia tamannu-ma
- -meš ta-sal-la-'

[End of the MAQLU series.]

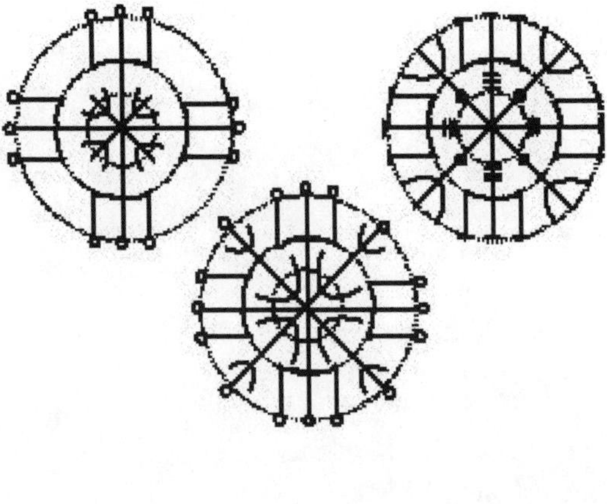

APPENDIX

Devils & Demons of Babylonia: *Leaves from the* NECRONOMICON ANUNNAKI BIBLE

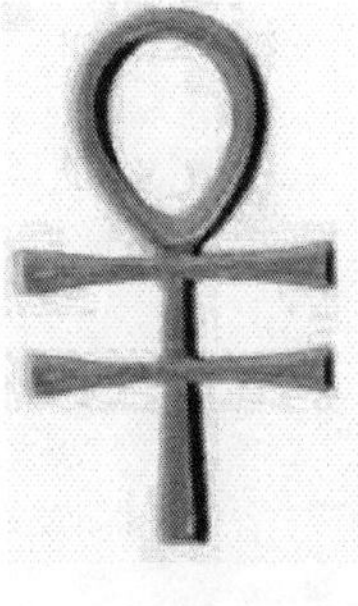

Tablet-H – Headaches & Demonologie

– from Liber 9 –

In the Babylonian system, the priesthood dedicated to the exorcisms and banishment of ill-fortune (thought to be brought on by the people's thoughts and deeds themselves, or those of another – e.g. wicked sorcerer) are called the "*asipu*" or "*masmasu*". While it has been thought that all forms of "witchcraft" and "sorcery" (essentially "magic") were deemed evil, this is not remotely the case. In addition to the obviously mystical nature of the priesthood, these "*wizards*" and "*witch-doctors*" were actually given a highly esteemed class-status of combating against the "evil" sorcery cast by the lower class "hostile" and "wicked" ones.

The "Words of Power" associated with both the subtle conjuring of the "*daemons*" or the violent exorcisms of the "evil genius" - whether it be by the most holy *Roman Catholic Ritulae* or the most diabolic of grimoires (e.g. the "*Grand Grimoire*" and "Dragon" grimiores – which occupy the same mythological paradigm as Catholicism and Judaism) are always of the "highest" - or else to say: "Holy Names" (e.g. Tetragrammaton). This is because the vibrations of the Material World occupy under the governance of the Material Ruler or Lord of the Earth, which may have appeared in the past as a "Source God" but of which is only a "cyclic god". Exceptions within this system are the co-creators of this system, which is not Absolute, but a separation or shadow from the whole.

It has always been the "Supernal Trinities" and "Unspeakable Names" that carries both the avenging hunter and the glorifying worshiper of the "*daemon*" shadow. And the wise appear to use the systematic hierarchy of the "highest" to achieve these ends. For in the ancient times we see the priests of Eridu and Babylon calling to Marduk to appeal to his farther Enki. By the time of the Jewish mystics, such as we find in the "*Book of Abramelin*", this title has been generalized to *Adonai*, meaning simply, *Lord of the Earth*, though fundamentalist monotheists can only perceive the notion as "God – Source." Catholic priests and Christian sciences have adopted the name of "Jesus" as *Adonai* for the *Piscean Age* (e.g. "Christ Consciousness"), something that occultists actually find logical.

No different then we find among the cornucopia of anecdotal paranormal experiences today, the ancients had their run-ins with what contemporary society once generalized as "ghosts" - meaning the ethereal spiritual presence of an ancestral ("dead") spirit, or rather an spirit that returns due to its "unrest" or difficulty in "crossing". These are called "*edimmu*" ("E.DI.IM.MI") in Babylonian (Assyrian) lexicons. Another is called the "*utukku*."

Although later interpreted to be a "daemon" (without being distinguished for its beneficent nature), the "*lamassu*" is a "positive" guardian spirit that is called forth in many of the tablet rites. It is hard to separate, in all cases, the difference between this spirit and the "*sedu*" guardian, but the combined lore of these led to the later Assyrian belief in "guardian angels" that was carried over into the Judeo-Christian beliefs until present times.

Although later interpreted to be a “daemon” (without being distinguished for its beneficent nature), the “*lamassu*” is a “positive” guardian spirit that is called forth in many of the tablet rites. It is hard to separate, in all cases, the difference between this spirit and the “*sedu*” guardian, but the combined lore of these led to the later Assyrian belief in “guardian angels” that was carried over into the Judeo-Christian beliefs until present times.

The role of “*sympathetic magic*” in these affects cannot be over-looked. Given the vivid descriptions we have been given to draw off from ancient tablets, we see evidence for the stereotypical “voodoo-doll” as perhaps the most ancient recorded “folk charm” - used to represent a psychic target for either side as they essentially may be used to curse or remove curses or heal. The role of “sympathetic magic” in these affects cannot be over-looked. Given the vivid descriptions we have been given to draw off from ancient tablets, we see evidence for the stereotypical “*voodoo-doll*” as perhaps the most ancient recorded “folk charm” - used to represent a psychic target for either side as they essentially may be used to curse or remove curses or heal.

Representative figures made of wax frequently appear. In fact the *Book of Burnings & the Maklu* can even be seen as a literal interpretation of the burning, melting, waxen images: “Ceremonial burnings in metaphoric effigy are usually performed with waxen dolls “made in the image of your enemy.” Elsewhere it explains that “a waxen doll may be cursed over a flame and then melted into a cauldron”. The idea of connecting to the spirit or “soul” of a being via some waxen or natural-made image can be connected to the mystical practices of the Babylonians, Egyptians and Semitic tribes.

The concept of cleanliness with sanity can be traced back to the roots of the word in Indo-European history, and to emphasize further the point, the ideas of uncleanliness, sin and demons are all synonymous among the ancients. The violation of health taboos also contributed to the connection between cleanliness and sin – though prior to these learned behaviors, the origins may have a much more ceremonial inclination – as described in Morgenstern's *Doctrine of Sin in the Babylonian Religion*: “the express-ions: sin, uncleanliness, sickness, possession by evil spirits, are pure synonyms. They denote an evil state of the body, the result of the divine anger...sin must have been originally purely ritual. Either the man had neglected to offer his sacrifice, or else had not offered it properly.” It is important to note that before the sacrifices could be offered properly, a person would have first needed a “ritual cleansing” - furthering again the combined significance.

Tablet-Y – Ceremonial Notes

– from Liber G –

This introductory rite is comparable to what many modern practitioners have encountered as the L.B.R.P (Lesser Banishing Ritual of the Pentagram). The rite is used often in contemporary ceremonial magick. A Mardukite version, also known as the "Priest's Incantation of Eridu," may be used within the ANUNNAKI system. The purpose of the rite is the same: a minor preliminary and closing rite used to banish the existing energies of the space, acknowledge the beings, consecrate the space as a "mandala" or magick circle to them, and finally to graciously negate the resonant ritual energies at the end.

In the L.B.R.P, blue or whitish pentagrams are traced and envisioned in addition to the activation of the elemental gates.

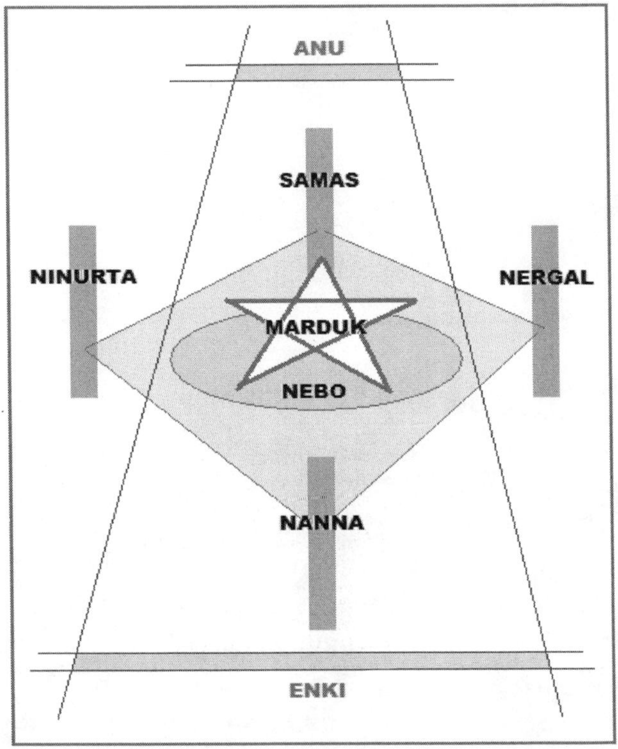

Egypto-Babylonian rituals from ancient times often involved lighting a lamp or lantern at each quarter as well as a larger central fire consecrated to the *fire god*. Candles may be substituted when necessary.

I am the priest of MARDUK, Son of our
Father, ENKI.
I am the priest in ERIDU and the
Magician in BABYLON.
SAMAS is before me.
NANNA-SIN is behind me.
NERGAL is at my right hand.
NINURTA is at my left hand.

About me flames the Pentagram, the Sign
of our Race,
Above and Below me shine the Ladder of
Lights.
ANU, Above me, the King in Heaven.
ENKI, Below me, the Lord of the Deep.

The Power of MARDUK is within me.
It is not I, but MARDUK, who commands
thee!

– SUPPLEMENTAL –
A CONJURATION (OF THE FIRE GOD)

Servant of the Great God, Companion of the
Flame,
Bringer of Light. GIRRA – GIBIL – NUSKU.
You, whose mouth is the Unquenchable
Flame,
You, who is seated in the Fire,

You, whose seat is in the Lake of Fire in
Heaven,
In whose hands is left the greatness and
power of God.
Reveal yourself here this day [night] and
speak with me,
And give me answer without falsehood.

I will glorify your name before the Sun.
I will glorify your name before the Moon.
Rise up, Son of the Flaming Disk of ANU.
Great God, ANU, Heavenly Father,
Descend into me with your Holy Servant, I
invoke thee.

GIBIL GASHRU UMUNA YANDURU TUSHTE
YESH SHIR ILLANI U MA YALKI – GISHBAR IA
ZI IA. ZI DINGIR GIRRA KANPA.

It is not I, but MARDUK, Slayer of Serpents
who calls thee here now.
It is not I, but ENKI, Father of the Magicians
who summons thee.

Come forth, in and give answer.
Come forth and let my eyes be opened this
day [night].
Spirit of the God of Fire, thou are conjured!

Additional recommended materials
by JOSHUA FREE

Necronomicon Anunnaki Bible
(Liber N,L,G,9 anthology)

Gates of the Necronomicon
(Liber 50,51,R anthology)

Sumerian Religion: Secrets of the Anunnaki
(Liber 50 standalone title)

Necronomicon Revelations
(Liber R standalone title)

Babylonian Myth & Magic
(Liber 51 standalone title)

The Book of Marduk by Nabu
(Liber/Tablet-W series)

MARDUKITE

2086384R00104

Made in the USA
San Bernardino, CA
09 March 2013